POPULAR
LITERATURES
IN AFRICA

BERNTH LINDFORS

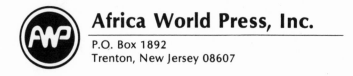

Africa World Press, Inc.

P.O. Box 1892
Trenton, New Jersey 08607

Africa World Press, Inc.
P.O. Box 1892
Trenton, NJ 08607

Library of Congress Catalog Card Number: 91-70721

ISBN: 0-86543-220-1 Cloth
0-86543-221-X Paper

Cover Design: Ife Nii-Owoo

Comparative Studies in African/Caribbean Literature Series

Series Editor: Stephen H. Arnold
Associate Editor: George Lang

African and Caribbean Literature Section
Research Institute for Comparative Literature
The University of Alberta
Edmonton, Alberta
CANADA T6G 2E6

Contents

Preface   v
Acknowledgements   vii
Introduction   1

WEST AFRICA

Ayi Kwei Armah's Histories   3
Chinua Achebe's African Parable   15
Postwar Popular Literature In Nigeria   23
The Rise of African Pornography   35

EAST AFRICA

Popular Literature in East Africa   47
The Songs of Okot p'Bitek   61
Petals of Blood as a Popular Novel   79
The New David Maillu   87

SOUTH AFRICA

Popular Literature in Black South Africa   101
Robin Hood Realism in South African Fiction   111
Dennis Brutus's Mousey Tongue: People's Poetry in Exile   117
Seeing the Races Through Zulu Spectacles   127

RICLAC

RICLAC

"RICLAC" (Research Institute for Comparative Literature — Africa/Caribbean) is a not for profit entity associated with the University of Alberta. RICLAC's purposes are:

— encouragement, publication and dissemination of high quality scholarship on Third World — especially African and Caribbean — cultural topics;

— occasional publication of original creative works by Third World authors;

— sponsorship of lectures, conferences and symposia;

— contribution to the training of graduate students, post-doctoral fellows and visiting research scholars at the University of Alberta;

— the nurturing of an awareness of practical development problems among scholars working in cultural realms; and

— contribution to the alleviation of the book famine in Africa by providing free copies of its publications to African and Caribbean research libraries. (RICLAC gratefully accepts Third World publications in exchange for its volumes.)

An Editorial Board of distinguished scholars from Africa, Europe and Latin and North America reviews all manuscripts. Authors whose works are published by RICLAC are expected to assist in gaining grants for RICLAC's Book Famine Project.

RICLAC's Director and Associate Director are Professors Stephen Arnold and George Lang of the Department of Comparative Literature, The University of Alberta, Edmonton T6G 2E6, Canada.

Preface

.

Just as outside of Africa where the masses of ordinary readers enjoy the popular varieties of literary potboilers more than the elitist, sanitized tomes studied in schools, so inside of Africa the general reading public is most absorbed by works which have aesthetics as only a peripheral concern. Yet in the realm of African literary scholarship, too little time has been spent exploring the wonderful popular underside of the literary pyramid. Here at last is an entire book on the topic, a collection of essays written by Bernth Lindfors over a period of some twenty years. When Lindfors told me not long ago that he was going to put together such a book, I jumped at the chance to publish it, for although anything by this leader in the field of anglophone African literary criticism is well worth publishing, I knew that this book would include some of his well known wit in its most potent expressions. In many ways the pieces he brought together are as "popular" as the works they explore. Although some of the essays are sober in a traditional academic style, many are frequently unorthodox in their irreverence, defying the genres of criticism devoted to the "higher" types of African literature in which so much has been written by hundreds of others as well as by Lindfors himself.

This project was finalized in October 1989 in Sweden, when Bernth Lindfors was laureled with an honorary doctorate by the University of Umeå near his place of birth. Part of the ceremonies surrounding that occasion included a two day Symposium on African Popular Culture. Organized by Raoul Granqvist, the Symposium drew scholars from many countries. During interludes in the highly solemn events outside the Symposium, and frequently during the Symposium itself, a great deal of fun was poked at "Ben" Lindfors by his many friends present, but the quiet Swedish-American always managed to draw the biggest laughs with his punning, ribald one-liners and extended, often silly, yet illuminating metaphors, with his ability to find scholarly fodder in the simultaneously sublime and ridiculous. It is a pleasure to present these essays to a broader public than that which has had access to them only in arcane scholarly journals, for it shows that a serious, neglected subject can be treated as something worthy of respect and of high scholarly contemplation without being emptied of its entertainment value. Here, then, is vintage Lindfors — controversial, provocative, historical, documentary, seminal, and often finding fun while always maintaining the highest standards of literary scholarship.

Stephen H. Arnold
University of Alberta

Acknowledgements

I wish to express my gratitude to the editor and publishers of *Africa Today*, *African Literature Today*, *Anglistik und Englischunterricht*, *Journal of Popular Culture*, *Journal of Southern African Affairs*, *Kunapipi*, *Okike*, *Présence Africaine*, *Transition*, *World Literature Written in English*, and of the books *Contemporary African Literature* and *The Writing of East and Central Africa* for allowing me to reprint material that first appeared in their pages. I also wish to thank the University Research Institute of The University of Texas at Austin, the National Endowment for the Humanities, and the ACLS/SSRC Joint Committee on African Studies for generously supporting my research on African popular literatures. In addition, I am extremely grateful to Stephen Arnold and Kassahun Checole, publishers of this volume, for their patience, perseverance, efficiency and helpfulness, but most of all, for their genial good humor, which made it a treat to work with them. More publishers should be so enjoyably popular.

Introduction

"Popular literature" can be a misleading term when applied to a body of writings from Africa. Obviously, in a continent with a high rate of illiteracy, no literature has a chance of reaching and pleasing a majority of the population. In Africa the situation is complicated further by a remarkable multiplicity of languages — more than a thousand in all, most of which have never been written down. In such circumstances it is impossible to conceive of any literature becoming truly "popular" in the sense of becoming known and appreciated by many millions of readers. In Africa popular literature is not mass literature because the masses either cannot all read the same language or else cannot read at all.

Those Africans who are literate tend to live and work in urban areas where they earn incomes considerably higher than the national average. Their education has prepared them for a style of life quite different from that of the unschooled peasant or common laborer. Except in the Muslim north, where Arabic remains the dominant medium of instruction, they have been exposed in school to a Western-style curriculum and have absorbed Western culture and Western habits while learning a Western language. They are an urbanized, acculturated elite, and their reading tastes tend to reflect their new interests and enthusiasms as well as their adjustment to conflicting sets of values and to modern city life. It is only among such people — a relatively small fraction of the total population — that it is possible to speak of the emergence of African popular literatures.

Of course, some Africans have had more formal education than others so a variety of "taste cultures"[1] may be found in any literate African society. Each of these will be characterized by its own entertainment preferences, its own favorite creative media, and hence its own distinctive forms of popular literature. Yet all literate members of an African society will be exposed to some of the same literary materials simply because these materials are more widely available than others. In certain areas, hardly any alternatives will exist. There is, in other words, a common denominator as well as a variable factor in the reading propensities of any African audience. A literature's "popularity" may be as much a function of such random circumstances as geography, economics, politics, and education as it is a manifestation of a particular group's aesthetic preferences.

The essays collected here deal with African works of fiction, poetry and drama that have achieved a measure of commercial success in Africa and

1

may also have attracted a sizable audience abroad. Nearly all these books, pamphlets and performances were created primarily for the entertainment and edification of their authors' literate, English-speaking compatriots, the exceptions being certain South African works directed of necessity toward foreign readers or spectators. One could argue that texts or shows that continue to be widely appreciated at home are more truly reflective of the "taste culture" emerging among educated elites in modern Africa than are indigenous works produced and consumed entirely overseas. Yet even art created in exile may express an authentically African experience in terms that can be universally understood, so a definition of African popular literature need not exclude what is written, read or performed outside Africa. A more satisfactory criterion would be the idiom in which the ideas are articulated. Any work that seeks to communicate an African perspective to a large audience in a style that can be readily apprehended and appreciated could legitimately be called a piece of African popular literature.

Thus, the novels of Armah, Achebe, and Ngugi, the short stories of La Guma, Rive, and Mphahlele, the poetry of p'Bitek, Mtshali and Brutus, the pornography of Osahon and Maillu, the pamphlet literature of Onitsha and Nairobi, and the Zulu musicals brought to London in the nineteenth and twentieth centuries can be discussed together as disparate manifestations of essentially the same creative impulse: the will to speak directly to as many people as possible. There is little obscurity or subterfuge in this kind of literature because the author is intent on making an immediate impact. He wants his art to be understood. Though he may aim his message principally at his countrymen, anyone who happens to be within earshot should be able to grasp what he is saying.

The role of the critic in dealing with such literature should be to set it in a context that will make its reverberations more meaningful. He should function as an amplifier of what is plain rather than as an interpreter of what is imagined to be concealed. Yet he should be careful not to confine his attention solely to bald surface realities, for even the most crudely crafted work may have interesting interior dimensions and deep layers of significance that contribute significantly to the vigor of its overall effect. The critic of popular literature must therefore probe as well as amplify his subject, bringing out the best and the worst in art that might otherwise be considered quite ordinary. Writing such criticism is not a trivial undertaking.

NOTE

1. For further elucidation of this concept, see Herbert J. Gans, *Popular Literature and High Culture: An Analysis and Evaluation of Taste* (New York: Basic Books, 1975).

Ayi Kwei Armah's Histories

When Ayi Kwei Armah went to live in Tanzania in 1970, some readers wondered what effect this move might have on his fiction. He had already registered his revulsion against human corruption in his native Ghana in the two anguished novels that had established his reputation as a significant writer, *The Beautyful Ones Are Not Yet Born* and *Fragments*, and in his next and perhaps most cynical work, *Why Are We So Blest?*, published in 1972,[1] he broadened the scope of his satire to include mortals elsewhere, particularly the featherbedded leaders of the revolutionary movement in Algeria and the naive, misguided, racist liberals, white and black, in the United States. It was clear that the attitudes informing these misanthropic narratives had been shaped by his own experiences in the three societies depicted; his years at Harvard, his return to Ghana, and his months in Algiers lay reflected in the background like subterranean raw material out of which valuable gems of social insight had been mined and brought to light. The question was: what would he dig up in Tanzania? What could he find to be disillusioned about there? What targets would he choose for his next attack?

There had been some concern expressed by African intellectuals that Armah's vision was warped, that his stony view of African society, though brilliantly lucid, perpetuated the kind of distortion of reality that had existed throughout the colonial era and could ultimately prove harmful to the African revolution. Ama Ata Aidoo, in the preface to the American edition of *The Beautyful Ones Are Not Yet Born*, complained that "whatever is beautiful and genuinely pleasing in Ghana or Ghanaians seems to have gone unmentioned"; some of Armah's countrymen, she said, "could find it difficult to accept in physical terms the necessity for hammering on every page the shit and stink from the people and the environment."[2] Ben Obumselu, commenting on the same novel, suggested that in his reaction to the offensive sights and smells of mother Africa, Armah was expressing "the aesthetic discomfort of an American tourist" and a "misanthropic neurosis" that was characteristic of an "exiled imagination."[3] Chinua Achebe said that he had found the first novel "a sick book"[4] and the second "worse than the first and the third...worse than the second"[5]; he described Armah as an "alienated native...writing like some white District Officer."[6] Toward what kind of social transformation, he asked, could a

3

writer overwhelmed by existential despair and such destructive, negative images of Africa be committed?[7]

Armah has now answered some of the questions raised about his art by writing two novels which attempt to put the accent on the positive. To do this, he has had to retreat into history, first into a figmental past stretching back a full millenium in *Two Thousand Seasons*,[8] then into the welldocumented events a century ago that led to the downfall of the Ashanti empire, as recreated in *The Healers*.[9] At a moment when other Africans writers were insisting that the creative artist come to terms with contemporary African realities, Armah appeared to be swimming against the tide by immersing himself in times gone by. Yet his was a Janus-like view, for it looked forward at the same time that it fixed its gaze on the past. In fact, these novels are really more concerned with tomorrow than with yesterday or today. They are visionary myths rather than historical chronicles.

It is tempting to read current Tanzanian political ideology into such fictions because the emphasis in both is on brotherhood, sharing, self-reliance and unity. Basic to the argument of each are certain philosophical assumptions: that wealth should be distributed equitably in a society, that the welfare of the community as a whole is more important than that of any single individual in it, that institutions of kingship, chieftaincy or any other arbitrary forms of hierarchial social order that place one man above others are unnatural and exploitative, that true socialism is, always has been, and ever shall be a guiding principle in indigenous African life. It looks almost as if Armah were trying to justify the ways of TANU to man by creating a legendary prehistory of Ujamaa.

The events recorded do not take place in East Africa, however. Both novels are set in West Africa, *The Healers* quite specifically in nineteenth century Ghana, *Two Thousand Seasons* more generally in a green area bounded on one side by a great desert and on the other by a great sea. The peoples living in this peaceful sub-Saharan haven are subjected to attacks from hostile strangers who invade their territory, taking advantage of their trustfulness, generosity, and the internal political divisions that make them vulnerable to foreign aggression. In other words, both books present Africa as a victim of outside forces that it resists but cannot contain. These depradations of the past are responsible for the chaos one sees in Africa at present, and only by properly understanding that past and present will Africans collectively be able to tackle the problems of the future; how to get the victim back on its feet, how to raise the materially oppressed and downtrodden, how to heal the spiritually sick. Instead of merely cursing various symptoms of the colonial disease, as he had done in his first three books, Armah now wants to work toward effecting a cure.

The strategy in *Two Thousand Seasons* is to take the longest possible view by moving backward in time to that distant point when an alien civilization first impinged upon African existence. According to Armah, this would have been the period of the Arab incursions into the Sudanic grasslands, the aboriginal home of happy, self-sufficient African communities. Armah calls the Arabs predators, saying they first came out of the desert in the guise of parasitic beggars and then, after being sustained and nursed to greater strength by their African hosts who were by nature noble, hospitable, and far too charitable, the Arabs turned their innate fury against these very benefactors, by massacring and enslaving them. The predators, their minds debased by a perverted religion, their bodies yearning for every variety of sybaritic self-gratification, were capable only of depravity and destruction. Whatever they touched, they maimed or killed. The Arab way was the way of annihilation, of absolute obliteration of all that was good, wholesome and creative. For them,

> force is goodness. Fraud they call intelligence...In their communion there is no respect, for to them woman is a thing, a thing deflated to fill each strutting, mediocre man with a spurious, weightless sense of worth. With their surroundings they know but one manner of relationship, the use of violence. Against other peoples they recommend to each other the practice of robbery, cheating, at best smiling at dishonesty. Among them the sphere of respect is so shrunken they themselves have become sharp-clawed desert beasts, preying against all.
>
> They plant nothing. They know but one harvest: rape. The work of nature they leave to others: the careful planting, the patient nurturing. It is their vocation to fling themselves upon the cultivator and his fruit, to kill the one, to carry off the other. Robbery with force: that is the predators' road, that is the white destroyers' road. (pp. 62-63)

Contact with so pathological an evil inevitably led some susceptible Africans to follow the predators' road. This they did by becoming devotees of the new religion, or by trying to raise themselves above others through displays of impressive splendor, or simply by enforcing the slave laws of the conquerors. Armah has a name for each traitorous group: the first he calls "zombis," the second "ostentatious cripples," the third "askari zombis." The initial schism in African society thus developed as a consequence of the Arab invasion and the concomitant spread of Islam. Africans who had been won over to the new faith or who had chosen to serve the conquerors turned against their own kith and kin.

The more resilient Africans, those who steadfastly refused to be converted or corrupted by the new forces in their world, decided that the best way to counter such disintegrative pressures was not to confront them in a suicidal counter-attack but rather to remove themselves from the sphere of their harmful influence. So a migration took place – long, arduous, lasting many seasons, covering great distances. Grassland gradually gave way to forest and swamp, and the pilgrims, archetypal refugees from religious and political oppression, finally reached their promised land a short distance from the sea. Here they hoped to be left undisturbed by marauders, but almost immediately they met a new alien force – the white invaders from the sea.

These European "destroyers" turned out to be even worse than the Arab "predators," for their unlimited greed was backed by a technology of death more devastating than anything Africa had previously known. At one point a spokesman summed up the base desires of these monsters:

> The white men wish us to destroy our mountains, leaving ourselves wastes of barren sand. The white men wish us to wipe out our animals, leaving ourselves carcasses rotting into white skeletons. The white men want us to take human beings, our sisters and our sons, and turn them into laboring things. The white men want us to take human beings, our daughters and our brothers, and turn them into slaves. The white men want us to obliterate our remembrance of our way, the way, and in its place to follow their road, road of destruction, road of a stupid childish god. (pp. 130-31)

To accomplish these goals the white men offered African kings and their courtiers worthless, glittering gifts, thereby bribing them with trinkets to collaborate in the enslavement of their own people.

The rest of the novel focuses on one small band of Africans who get sold to European slave traders but stage a successful shipboard revolt and then form themselves into a pioneer liberation army which wreaks vengeance against the white destroyers and their black lackeys. This group of guerillas, self-trained and splendidly disciplined, dedicate themselves to the destruction of Africa's enemies, the most creative vocation possible for freedom fighters intent on purging their world of the debilitating malignancies inflicted upon it by European and Arab imperialism.

It is an interesting scenario and a fascinating contrast to Armah's earlier fiction. Instead of watching one man struggle fruitlessly to maintain his purity or sanity in an atmosphere of rank corruption, we see a communal group, activitated by the highest ideals, actually *succeed* in their military maneuvers against extraordinarily powerful antagonists. Instead of witnessing the anguish of a doomed, fragmented individual, we are shown the joy of a mini-tribe united in the struggle against evil. Instead of existential despair, there is revolutionary hope. Instead of defeat, victory.

But the optimism in Armah's new view of man and society in Africa is predicated on certain assumptions which it is difficult to credit as reasonable. Foremost among these is the belief that Africa, before being polluted by contact with the outside world, was a Garden of Eden, at least in terms of social organization. People lived in harmonious communities, sharing the fruits of their labor and never striving to compete against their neighbors for the acquisition of superior status or material goods. Rulers did not exist; the communities were acephalous, completely democratic, and devoted to the principle of reciprocity. This principle was the very essence of what Armah calls "our way, the way." Here it is in one of its most compact formulations:

> Our way is reciprocity. The way is wholeness. Our way knows no oppression. The way destroys oppression. Our way is hospitable to guests. The way repels destroyers. Our way produces before it consumes. Our way creates. The way destroys only destruction. (p. 62)

So Africans were a creative, productive, hospitable, non-oppressive, healthy and sharing people – until the invaders came. Africans should now strive to return to "our way, the way" by destroying the destroyers of their former paradise.

The villains in this stark melodrama are portrayed as the obverse of the heroes. This may be a dramatic necessity, inasmuch as one needs very potent Manichean forces to overwhelm such a superabundance of virtue as is said to have existed in prehistoric Africa. But it also assumes that entire races of people can be reduced to the level of primal forces, that one can be characterized as inherently predisposed towards good, another addicted to evil. This kind of xenophobic oversimplification used to be found in B-grade films manufactured in Hollywood during the Second World War, in which fanatical Kamikaze pilots and fat, stupid, goose-stepping German generals represented all that was reprehensible in the world. The "Japs" and "Krauts" in such celluloid fantasies performed essentially the same function as the "predators" and "destroyers" in Armah's fiction: they were crude, simplistic symbols toward which a chauvinistic audience could direct the energy of its hatred while waiting for the satisfying denouement in which vice would be vanquished and virtue rewarded. The good guys might lose a few battles but they always won the war.

The trouble with Armah's cartoon history of Africa is that it ultimately is not a positive vision, even though it promises future happiness. All it really offers is negation of negation. The most creative act imaginable is destruction of the destroyers. The last pages of *Two Thousand Seasons* reiterate this theme with evangelical fervor:

> Destruction of destruction is the only vocation of the way... The liberator is he who from a necessary silence, from a necessary secrecy strikes the destroyer... Nothing good can be created that does not of its very nature push forward the destruction of the destroyers... Whatever thing, whatever relationship, whatever consciousness takes us along paths closer to our way, whatever goes against the white destroyers' empire, that thing only is beautiful, that relationship only is truthful, that consciousness alone has satisfaction for the still living mind. (pp. 316-20)

This is a philosophy of paranoia, an anti-racist racism – in short, Negritude reborn. In place of a usable historical myth, *Two Thousand Seasons* over-schematizes the past, creating the dangerous kind of lie that Franz Fanon used to call a "mystification."

Compare, for example, Armah's treatment of history with Chinua Achebe's. In *Things Fall Apart* and *Arrow of God* Achebe shows us complex human beings entangled in a web of circumstances that ultimately brings disaster to rural Igbo society. The individuals portrayed cannot be divided into two camps – the saints versus the sinners – but rather can be recognized as quite ordinary people motivated by fairly commonplace ambitions and desires. Moreover, the communities in which they live are not perfect or even remotely perfectible; they are rife with conflicts ranging from the petty to the profound, conflicts which are exacerbated when an alien civilization intrudes into their relatively encapsulated world. The ensuing interaction between Europe and Africa is not really a species of all-out war but rather an uneasy, and at times unpeaceful, coexistence of differing worldviews in which the inability of one side to comprehend the perspective of the other precipitates tragedy. Achebe perceives that it was a failure of communication, not an absence of humaity, that was responsible for certain of the catastrophes of the colonial period. In documenting the numerous ironies of this confused era with such compassion and lucidity, Achebe proves a more convincing historian than Armah. Achebe deeply understands ethnocentrism, whereas Armah shallowly advocates it.

In his latest novel, *The Healers*, Armah moves a step closer to fleshing out his nightmare vision of the past by substituting concrete substance for abstract symbol. If *Two Thousand Seasons* was his theory of history, *The Healers* is an adumbration of the theory using actual recorded events as proofs of the hypotheses advanced. Armah takes the fall of the Ashanti empire as emblematic of Africa's destruction, and he attributes the calamity not only to the rapacity of the West but also to the disunity within Africa itself. It is toward the reunification of Africa tomorrow that Africans must work today if they wish to repair the damage done yesterday. History is again seen as a guide to a better future.

The novel itself is unified by the imagery of disease. Africa has been prostrated by a foreign plague against which it had no natural immunity, and some of its members, infected beyond all possibility of recovery, have turned against the parent body itself, spreading the disabling disorder still further. Any manifestation of division in society is regarded as a symptom of the malady, a crippling indisposition requiring a cure.

Notice how smoothly this imagery of illness is employed to elucidate Armah's underlying political philosophy in the following passage:

> Healing an individual person – what is that but restoring lost unity to that individual's body and spirit?
>
> A people can be diseased the same way. Those who need naturally to be together but are not, are they not a people sicker than the individual body disintegrated from its soul? Sometimes a whole people needs healing work. Not a tribe, not a nation. Tribes and nations are just signs that the whole is diseased. The healing work that cures a whole people is the highest work, far higher than the cure of single individuals...
>
> The ending of all unnatural rifts is healing work. When different groups within what should be a natural community clash against each other, that also is disease. That is why healers say that our people, the way we are now divided into petty nations, are suffering from a terrible disease. (pp. 100-1)

Fortunately, there are a few remarkably perceptive hermits living a pure life on the fringes of this sick society who are devoted to the art of healing. They function simultaneously as physicians, psychoanalysts, and social theorists, for they are committed not only to restoring the physical and mental health of ailing individuals but also to purging the body politic of all its ills. Because they possess the ability to see, hear, understand and act more truly than ordinary human beings, they are the seers and prophets who can lead Africa back to wholeness.

> A healer needs to see beyond the present and tomorrow. He needs to see years and decades ahead. Because healers work for results so firm they may not be wholly visible till centuries have flowed into millenia. Those willing to do this necessary work, they are the healers of our people. (p. 102)

Naturally, Densu, the hero of the novel, is one of these, or rather is an idealistic young man who, aspiring to join this elite fraternity, begins to undergo the long process of initiation and apprenticeship required. Certainly he seems to have all the necessary qualifications. Intelligent, sensitive, honest, courageous, hardy, persevering, self-sacrificing, totally dedicated, yet becomingly modest about his many prodigious achievements, he is the model pre-med student, the pluperfect seer-in-training. One searches in vain for the tiniest flaw in his character.

At this point one is tempted to pause and ask why so many of Armah's heroes are of this saintly breed? Why does he feel compelled to make his protagonists supermen? Are such beautiful ones ever born? Is Armah bent on creating a new type of utopian fiction? Or is he merely rewriting a modern secular version of *The Pilgrim's Progress* in which an upright un-Christian soldier, beset by numerous temptations, goes singlemindedly marching on to social salvation, never veering from the straight and narrow path, "our way, the way?"

Densu, a bit younger than most of Armah's puritanical protagonists, is introduced to us as an unsullied boy scout. In village games testing physical and mental prowess, he invariably is the overall champion, losing only when he defaults by refusing to participate in wrestling and pigeon shooting – violent sports that violate his higher moral principles. It is true that he is beaten in a few short sprints by a more muscular Adonis, but he reigns supreme in the long distance races demanding greater stamina and controlled efficiency of effort. However, even though he is a consistent winner, he dislikes such competitions because they set one individual against another – indeed, against his whole community. Densu, you see, believes in equality, brotherhood and reciprocity, not in individual achievement. But Armah lets us know that there is no prize, no merit badge that this paragon, born of noble blood, could not win if he really wanted to. Some socialists, as Orwell pointed out long ago, are more equal than others.

Densu serves his apprenticeship under Damfo, a master healer and supreme scoutmaster who lives, significantly, in the *eastern* forest. Damfo teaches him the seven commandments of the healer's faith and helps him to distinguish between two crucial concepts: "inspiration" and "manipulation."

> The healer devotes himself to inspiration. He also lives against manipulation [which is] a disease, a popular one. It comes from spiritual blindness. If I'm not spiritually blind, I see your spirit. I speak to it if I want to invite you to do something with me. If your spirit agrees it moves your body and your body acts. That's inspiration. But if I'm blind to your spirit I see only your body. Then if I want you to do something for me I force or trick your body into doing it even against your spirit's direction. That's manipulation. Manipulation steals a person's body from his spirit, cuts the body off from its own spirit's direction. The healer is a lifelong enemy of all manipulation. The healer's method is inspiration. (p. 99)

The major manipulators, of course, are the local court politicians and foreign imperialists whose greed is dividing Africa against itself. Discord and disunity are seen as by-products of the kind of political system that sets one man above others, that concentrates power in the hands of a few. Even the healers themselves are cautioned by Damfo against the dangers of elitism and power politics in their own work.

> We healers do not fear power. We avoid power deliberately, as long as that power is manipulative power. There is a kind of power we would all embrace and help create. It is the same power we use in our work: the power of inspiration. The power that respects the spirit in every being, in every thing, and lets every being be true to the spirit within. Healers should embrace that kind of power. Healers should help create that kind of power. But that kind of power – the power that comes from inspiration – can never be created with manipulators. If we healers allow the speedy results of manipulation to attract us, we shall destroy ourselves and more than ourselves, our vocation... Are we forgetting that for healers the meaning of the span of life takes in our whole people, not just our single separate lives? (p. 329)

So the struggle continues, not just here and now, but for generations to come. It may take another two thousand seasons for Africa to be healed through the power of inspiration.

It is clear that Armah himself wants to assist in the healing process. The role of the writer, he seems to be saying, is to inspire Africa to be true to its own spirit so it can be reunited as the harmonious community it once was before the predators and destroyers came. This is a noble goal, even if the "paradise lost" theme is a bit naive as an interpretation of human history. Armah evidently is trying to do something constructive in his fiction, something far more positive than he had done in his first three novels. Giving Africa a new, clean image of itself is a much more wholesome occupation than rubbing its nose in shit.

And, indeed, *The Healers* is a better balanced book, a saner piece of fiction, than *Two Thousand Seasons*. Gone, but not totally forgotten, are the Arab and European demons who were objects of such intense hatred in Armah's earlier venture into history. Gone, too, are the scenes of sexual perversion and the almost Homeric descriptions of bloodshed, gore and corporeal mutilation, descriptions which told in gleeful, gloating detail exactly where a bullet or blade entered an enemy's body and where it exited. Gone as well are the over-idealized band of forest guerrillas, those glamorous outlaws descended from a romantic blend of Mao, Mau Mau and Robin Hood, who, instead of offering the reader some semblance of fidelity to African life, gave imaginary life to African fidelity. Gone, in short, are the delerious fantasies that pushed *Two Thousand Seasons* beyond the dimensions of viable myth into the wilder liberties of lunatic nightmare.

The Healers, it must be admitted, also has its good and bad guys, its heavy-handed moralizing, and its propensity to force history to fit a predetermined ideological paradigm, but it is not a harmful book to put into the hands of young people. For one thing, it does not encourage xenophobia. For another, it emphasizes creativity ("inspiration") rather than destruction. And by concentrating on real events and weaving fiction into the fabric of fact, it helps young Africans to reshape their perspective on the past and come to a better understanding of the world in which they currently live. In other words, it offers an interpretation of human experience that seems valid because it is rooted in an imaginable reality.

Yet it is still a cartoon, still comic strip history. It will not persuade many adults because it falsifies far more than it authenticates and in the process fails to avoid the pitfalls of oversimplification. Nevertheless, some grown-ups will be able to enjoy it at the level of popular fiction, for it is good cops-and-robbers, cowboys-and-indians stuff. It even includes a murder mystery to bait the readers' interest. But basically it is juvenile adventure fiction of the *Treasure Island* or *King Solomon's Mines* sort, the only major difference being that it is thoroughly *African* juvenile adventure fiction. Densu is the new Jim Hawkins or Allan Quatermain, the young man with whom generations of schoolchildren will readily be able to identify. And he is a fine model for them, a decent and wholesome youth who, as Mark Twain is alleged to have said of James Fenimore Cooper's heroes, never gets his hair mussed and never farts. If the mission schools could somehow manage to forgive or forget Densu's tumbles in the grass with Ajoa, sales to high schools could be quite brisk. It might even become a set book for school certificate exams.

I am not saying this to belittle the novel's importance. Obviously, *The Healers* is a major attempt by a major African writer to reinterpret a major event in African history. But I think it will have its major impact on young people, and this is as it should be in any remythologizing of Africa. One must aim at winning the hearts and minds of the young, imbuing them with the highest ideals, and making them proud and happy to be Africans. This *The Healers* does better than any other novel Armah has written. And this is why it is potentially his most important book and certainly his healthiest. One can no longer complain that his vision is warped, his art sick.

So the Tanzanian years have been good ones for Armah, helping him to emerge from the destructive negativity of cynicism and despair, turning him in a more confident, affirmative direction. The would-be healer gives signs of having himself been cured. One waits now to see what the Lesotho years will bring.

NOTES

1.   This novel, which Armah started writing in Ghana in the mid-1960s, was not completed until after he had arrived in Tanzania in August 1970. Since it was published in 1972, and since Armah began writing *Two Thousand Seasons* in October 1971, one can assume that much of *Why Are We So Blest?* had been written in the 1960s and that Armah was able to finish it during his first year in Tanzania. In other words, it does not owe its inspiration to his Tanzanian experience in quite the same way as the next two novels apparently do.

Biographical information on Armah can be found in his essay, "Larsony, or Fiction as Criticism of Fiction," *First World* 1, 2 (1977): 50-55. This essay has been reprinted in *Asemka* 4 (1976): 1-14; *New Classic* 4 (1977): 33-45; and *Positive Review* 1 (1978): 11-14. The period during which *Two Thousand Seasons* (Nairobi: East African Publishing House, 1973) was written is recorded on page 321 of that novel.

2.   Ama Ata Aidoo, "Introduction," *The Beautyful Ones Are Not Yet Born* (New York: Collier-Macmillan, 1969), p. xii.

3.   Ben Obumselu, "Marx, Politics and the African Novel," *Twentieth Century Studies*, 10 (1973): 114-16.

4.   Chinua Achebe, "Africa and Her Writers," *Morning Yet on Creation Day* (London: Heinemann, 1975), p. 25. The same essay appears in a slightly different form in *In Person: Achebe, Awoonor and Soyinka at the University of Washington*, ed. Karen Morell (Seattle: African Studies Program, Institute for Comparative and Foreign Area Studies, University of Washington, 1975), pp. 3-23.

5.   "Class Discussion," in Morell, p. 52.

6.   Achebe, p. 26; Morell, pp. 15-16.

7.   Chinua Achebe, "Panel on Literature and Commitment in South Africa," *Issue*, 6, 1 (1976): 37.

8.   *Two Thousand Seasons* (Nairobi: East African Publishing House, 1973). All quotations are taken from this edition.

9.   *The Healers* (Nairobi: East African Publishing House, 1978). All quotations are taken from this edition.

Chinua Achebe's African Parable

Chinua Achebe's fourth novel, *A Man of the People*, details the rise and demise of "Chief the Honourable Dr. M. A. Nanga, M.P., L.L.D.," a corrupt, wheeling-dealing, opportunistic semi-literate who elbows his way to a lucrative ministerial post in the Government of an unnamed independent African country, uses his power and newly-acquired wealth to ensure his re-election, and is shaken from his lofty, befouled perch only when a group of idealistic young military officers topples the "fat-dripping, gummy eat-and-let-eat regime" by launching a sudden *coup d'état*. The novel, published just nine days after the first military coup in Nigeria, has been hailed by many reviewers[1] as a "prophetic" work, one in which Achebe predicted with uncanny accuracy the end of his country's First Republic.

Certainly the accuracy of Achebe's vision cannot be disputed. It was a rather eerie experience to read the last chapter of this novel in the early months of 1966 when Achebe's descriptions of fictional events seemed to correspond so closely to newspaper accounts of what was happening in Nigeria. For example, the coup was said to have been touched off by post-election turmoil:

> What happened was simply that unruly mobs and private armies having tasted blood and power during the election had got out of hand and ruined their masters and employers. (p. 162)[2]... The rampaging bands of election thugs had caused so much unrest and dislocation that our young Army officers seized the opportunity to take over. (p. 165)

The aftermath of the fictional coup corresponded with reality too.

> ...the military regime had just abolished all political parties in the country and announced they would remain abolished "until the situation became stabilized once again." They had at the same time announced the impending trial of all public servants who had enriched themselves by defrauding the state. The figure involved was said to be in the order of fifteen million pounds. (pp. 165-66)
>
> Overnight everyone began to shake their heads at the excesses of the last regime, at its graft, oppression and corrupt government: newspapers, the radio, the hitherto silent intellectuals and civil servants – everybody said what a terrible lot; and it became public opinion the next morning. (p. 166)

It was passages such as these that made Achebe appear a seer.

Yet I would like to argue that despite these seemingly clairvoyant passages, *A Man of the People* is not and was not meant to be a prophetic novel. Indeed, given the circumstances in Nigeria during the time Achebe was writing, *A Man of the People* should be recognized as a devastating satire in which Achebe heaped scorn on independent Africa by picturing one part of it just as it was. I believe Achebe ended the novel with a military coup in order to enlarge the picture to include Nigeria's neighbors, many of which had experienced coups. By universalizing the story in this way Achebe could suggest to his countrymen that what had happened in other unstable independent African countries might easily have happened in Nigeria too. The coup was meant as an African parable, not a Nigerian prophecy.

The manuscript of *A Man of the People* was submitted to Achebe's publisher in February, 1965,[3] and the book was published in London eleven months later on January 24, 1966.[4] Achebe's third novel, *Arrow of God*, had been submitted to this publisher in February, 1963[5] and had been published March 3, 1964. Since it is unlikely that Achebe began *A Man of the People* until he had completed *Arrow of God*, it is probably safe to assume that *A Man of the People* was written sometime between February, 1963 and February, 1965. There is good evidence that he was at work on the novel early in 1964.[6] During this period he was also working as Director of External Broadcasting for the Nigerian Broadcasting Company, a job that would have kept him abreast of the latest news.

Politics dominated the news in Nigeria at this time. By February, 1963, the seven-month state of emergency in the Western region had ended, and Chief Obafemi Awolowo and twenty-nine others had been arrested and charged with conspiring to overthrow the Federal Government by force. In September, 1963, Awolowo and nineteen others were convicted of treasonable felony and imprisoned. On October 1, 1963 Nigeria became a Federal Republic. Then, because of the doubtful accuracy of the official results of the 1962 census, which were never publicly released, a new census was taken in November, 1963. Since regional representation in the Federal Government was to be determined by the results of this census, politicians were eager that every one of their constituents be counted at least once. When the bloated preliminary results of the census were released in February, 1964, they were rejected by the Eastern and Midwestern Regions and protest demonstrations were held. On March 25, 1964, an editorial in the Lagos *Daily Times* warned that "The Federal Republic of Nigeria faces the grave danger of disintegration" because of the census crisis.

Worse times were yet to come. A Federal Election was due before the year was out, and political campaigning gradually grew more and more vicious. One observer reports that "Countless acts of political violence and thuggery occurred almost daily throughout the campaign, but notably increased during the last few weeks."[7] Electioneering irregularities were so frequent and widespread that one of the major political parties, the United Progressive Grand Alliance, announced that it would boycott the elections. This precipitated another crisis, for President Nnamdi Azikiwe, judging the election invalid, refused to call upon victorious Prime Minister Abubakar Tafawa Balewa to form a new government. For five days the country teetered on the brink of political chaos. On January 4, 1965, Azikiwe and Balewa finally reached a compromise and Azikiwe announced to the country that Balewa would form a "broadly-based national Government." By-elections were to be held in constituencies where elections had been totally boycotted, and allegations of fraud and intimidation were to be reviewed by the courts.

It should be remembered that Achebe's publisher received the manuscript of *A Man of the People* one month after this period of crisis and compromise. Achebe must have been working on the last chapters of the novel, which dramatize the turbulence and violence of an election campaign, during the months just preceding the Nigerian election. He was obviously drawing much of his inspiration from daily news reports. The last pages of the novel, those which describe the coup, must have been written very close to the time of the five day crisis following the election. What relevance this has to my argument I shall attempt to demonstrate in a moment.

First, however, let us look at the role of the Nigerian military force before, during and immediately after the 1964 election campaign. Before the campaign they had been used to restore civil order both at home and abroad. In December, 1960, Nigerian troops had been sent to the newly independent Republic of the Congo (Leopoldville) to help United Nations forces keep order, and in April, 1964, they had been dispatched to Tanganyika to relieve British troops who had put down a Tanganyikan Army mutiny. In Nigeria, Army troops had quelled a Tiv riot in 1960 and had maintained order in the Western region during the 1962 state of emergency. During the 1964 election campaign they were ordered to put down another Tiv riot and did so at the cost of 700 lives.[8] Throughout the campaign large squads of riot police were deployed to battle the thugs and hooligans hired by political candidates to terrorize their opposition. During the post-election crisis, troops were called out to safeguard the residences of Azikiwe and Balewa in Lagos and the cell of Awolowo in Calabar. Thus, before, during and after the 1964 election campaign the Nigerian Army played a prominent role as a peace-keeping force in Nigeria and abroad.

During this same period armies in many other African countries had acted as a disruptive force. In 1963 there were military coups in Togo, Congo-Brazzaville and Dahomey, and a military plot to assassinate President

Tubman was uncovered in Liberia. In 1964 there were army mutinies in Tanganyika, Uganda and Kenya, a revolution in Zanzibar, attempted coups in Gabon and Niger, and continued confusion and disorder in Congo-Leopoldville. On February 21, 1964, an editorial in the Lagos *Daily Times* deplored the use of bullets instead of ballots in French West Africa, and four days later the same paper remarked that "The constant cataclysms which have recently disrupted peace and order in Africa have produced a dangerous trend towards replacing the growing pattern of parliamentary rule with military juntas." Notice that at this time the trend toward military coups was regarded as "dangerous."

By the end of the year the mood of the country had changed considerably. The electioneering abuses, the breakdown of law and order, the numerous crises and compromises had produced a general distrust of politicians and a disillusionment with democratic processes of government. In a nationwide broadcast on December 10, 1964, President Azikiwe himself predicted the end of democracy in Nigeria:

> ...I have one advice to give to our politicians; if they have decided to destroy our national unity, then they should summon a roundtable conference to decide how our national assets should be divided, before they seal their doom by satisfying their lust for office...Should politicians fail to heed this warning, then I will venture a prediction that the experiences of the Democratic Republic of the Congo (Leopoldville) will be child's play if it ever comes to our turn to play such a tragic role.[9]

After the elections Azikiwe lamented that

> People in this country now evince a mood of weariness and frustration that is a sad contrast to the elation and confidence with which we ushered in independence barely four years ago. Far from presenting a united front, our country now shows a pattern of disintegration.[10]

The people themselves expressed their discontent with politicians in no uncertain terms. During the election crisis Lazarus Okeke wrote a letter to the Lagos *Daily Times* asserting that

> ...no well-wisher of Nigeria would recommend a blow-up of the country just because certain politicians cannot have their demand [sic] met. The welfare of the people as a nation definitely superceeds [sic] in importance the various vain and sectional claims of erring politicians.[11]

An unsigned article in the Lagos *Sunday Express* of January 1, 1965 went a step further:

Democracy has bred corruption in our society on a scale hitherto unknown in human history.

Nigeria needs a strong man with a strong hand. By this I mean, that Nigeria needs to be disciplined. Nigeria needs too be drilled.

The leadership we want is the leadership of a benevolent dictator who gets things done, not that of "democractic administrators" who drag their feet.

It is clear that a number of Nigerians would have welcomed a military coup in January, 1965. Indeed, several days after Azikiwe and Balewa had worked out their compromise, one disgruntled Easterner writing in Enugu's *Nigerian Outlook* expressed regret that the compromise had not been forestalled by military intervention:

> If civil strife had broken out on December 30, the armed forces might have gone into action as a last resort, and the President and Prime Minister might never have had an opportunity for negotiations.[12]

If further evidence is required to prove that many Nigerians had entertained the notion of a military coup during the election crisis, one need only turn to the Lagos *Sunday Times* of February 28, 1965, and read the text of an interview with Major-General Aguiyi-Ironsi who on February 15th of that year had been appointed the first Nigerian Commander of the Nigerian Army.[13] The interviewer tried to draw out Ironsi's views on the desirability of military intervention in state affairs in times of political turmoil, but Ironsi carefully side-stepped the questions.

> Had you been the Officer Commanding the Nigerian Army during the constitutional crisis resulting from the Federal elections last December, what would you have done?
>
> *Ironsi*: You mean, militarily or what?
>
> Both militarily or otherwise.
>
> *Ironsi*: I think what we should get clear is that the crisis was a political crisis...It did not require military action. . .It was a political thing, solved in a political way.
>
> Tell me, if there is a war, would you fight – out of conviction or would you carry out the orders of the government regardless as to which side is right or wrong?
>
> *Ironsi*:...I think it is true to say that any Army goes to war for justification...The job of the Army is to defend the country, no questions asked.
>
> Now, supposed it is an internal war...
>
> *Ironsi*: ...I don't know what you are trying to get at. . .Whatever you might have in mind, THE ARMY SUPPORTS THE GOVERNMENT THAT IS!
>
> If you were General Mobutu, how would you effect a solution [to the Congo impasse]?
>
> *Ironsi*: I'm not. I should wait till I'm confronted with such a situation.

That such questions could be asked and such cautious answers given eight weeks after the crisis suggests that the idea of a military resolution to Nigeria's political problems had occurred to many Nigerians other than Achebe and that it was still quite a live issue.

Seen in this light Achebe's "prophecy" appears much less prophetic. He had only foreseen what many others, including President Azikiwe, had foreseen or had hoped to see. A military coup was not necessarily "inevitable" in 1964-5 but it was regarded by a number of intelligent observers[14] as one of the few options left for a nation on the brink of anarchy. In a later interview Achebe put it this way:

> ...things had got to such a point politically that there was no other answer – no way you could resolve this impasse politically. The political machine had been so abused that whichever way you pressed it, it produced the same results; and therefore another force just had to come in. Now when I was writing *A Man of the People* it wasn't clear to me that this was going to be necessarily a military intervention. It could easily have been civil war, which in fact it very nearly was in Nigeria.[15]

Achebe chose a military coup as the most appropriate ending for his story and eleven months later Nigeria happened to make the same choice to close out one of the ugliest chapters in its history.

To interpret the military coup in *A Man of the People* as a prophecy is to suggest that Achebe meant the novel to relate only to Nigeria. This, I think, is a mistake. While it is evident that the novel owes much to what Achebe had observed in his own country, many of the events described had happened and were happening in other independent African countries. By ending with a coup, an event anticipated yet unknown in Nigeria but familiar elsewhere in Africa, Achebe added a dimension of universality to his story. It was no longer merely a satire on Nigeria but a satire on the rest of independent Africa as well. If the coup had a special meaning for Nigeria in the mid-sixties, it also contained a relevant moral for other emerging African nations wracked by internal political upheavals. The ending was meant to be true to Africa and not merely truthful about Nigeria. The coup was an African parable, not a Nigerian prophecy.

One of the most remarkable features of Chinua Achebe's fiction is that it never fails to transcend the local and particular and enter realms of universal significance. Achebe once said,

> After all the novelist's duty is not to beat this morning's headline in topicality, it is to explore *in depth* the human condition. In Africa he cannot perform this task unless he has a proper sense of history.[16]

The ending of *A Man of the People* reveals that Achebe has a proper sense of contemporary African history.

NOTES

1. See, e.g. Robert Green, *Nation*, April 18, 1966, pp. 465-66; D.A.N. Jones, *New Statesman*, January 28, 1966, pp. 132-33; *Times Literary Supplement*, February 3, 1966, p. 77; *Time*, August 19, 1966, p. 80.

2. All quotations are taken from *A Man of the People* (London: Heinemann, 1966).

3. Letter from W. Roger Smith of William Heinemann Ltd., London.

4. *Ibid.*

5. Chinua Achebe, "The Role of the Writer in a New Nation," *Nigeria Magazine*, 81 (June 1964): 158.

6. Richard Harris, "Nigeria: Crisis and Compromise," *Africa Report*, 10, 2 (March 1965): 27.

7. Billy Dudley gives this figure in "Violence in Nigerian Politics," *Transition*, 5, 21 (1965): 22.

8. *Nigerian Outlook*, December 11, 1964, p. 3.

9. *Nigerian Outlook*, January 4, 1965, p. 4.

10. January 1, 1965, p. 4.

11. January 16, 1965, p. 3.

12. It is perhaps significant and – considering what happened in January, 1966 – certainly ironic that during the election crisis Ironsi led the troops that guarded Prime Minister Balewa's home.

13. See, e.g. Billy Dudley, *op. cit.*, p. 33.

14. *Cultural Events in Africa*, 28 (March 1967), ii.

15. "The Role of the Writer in a New Nation," *Nigeria Magazine*, 81 (June 1964), 157.

Postwar Popular Literature In Nigeria

It is already clear that the Nigerian civil war has profoundly altered the course of Nigerian literary history. Many established authors who used to be preoccupied with the themes of colonial culture conflict or post-independence corruption have recently published novels, autobiographies, plays and poems based on real or imagined wartime experiences. The majority of the new writers who have emerged in the years since hostilities ended in January, 1970, have also been concerned with documenting the social and psychological consequences of military conflict. Even children's books have dealt frankly with civil war themes.[1]

The writers who appear to have been affected most by the war are Igbos who lived in Biafra while the fighting was going on. Among these, Chinua Achebe, Cyprian Ekwensi, John Munonye and the late Christopher Okigbo (who was killed while serving as a Major in the Biafran Army) are probably the best known outside Nigeria, but there are many others with hard-earned local reputations who have contributed their creative energies to the postwar literary reorientation, too. They have done this by writing pamphlets which have been printed, published, and sold in cities and towns trhoughout what came to be called the East Central State of the Federal Republic of Nigeria. They are lowbrow authors using a popular medium to communicate with the common man.[2]

Before the war the hub of the Nigerian popular publishing industry was Onitsha, a large commercial center on the Niger River. The famous market at Onitsha, purportedly "the largest market in the world,"[3] was flattened by repeated shelling in 1967, but after the Biafran capitulation Onitsha quickly reestablished itself as a major trading center and a new market was soon under construction. Although several of the major pamphlet publishers suffered great losses during the war and went into other lines of business afterwards, at least seven returned to Onitsha and started their presses rolling again.[4] By 1973 an Igbo scholar could report that Onitsha market literature was alive and well once more; those who had prematurely bemoaned its death, he said, were unaware of one vital fact; that the vast majority of the publishers of Onitsha market hail from those areas of southeastern Nigeria often referred to as the "Igbo Heartland." Their homes were thus never directly affected by the fighting, and they were able to preserve a good percentage of their book stocks. The moaners probably also lost sight of the quality of resilience which the Igbo-speaking people are believed to possess in abundance.

A visit to Onitsha today will convince the moaners that far from being "dead," Onitsha market literature not only is very much alive, but is likely to grow as a result of recent events in Nigeria. By October, 1970, five of the established publishers had opened impressive bookshops in which they sold remaining stocks and textbooks. But with only two presses functioning in Onitsha at the time, some of the publishers may have had secret fears about the future.

More than thirty-six months after the end of the war, the situation is entirely different. There are over one hundred presses in Onitsha, and these are sometimes so busy that Onitsha pamphlets have to be printed at presses located in Nnewi and Orlu, 15 and 35 miles respectively south of Onitsha. [5]

The initial tendency of these publishers was to issue reprints of titles which had sold well before the war, titles which had come to be known in the Onitsha book trade as "evergreens." One soon found new editions of a whole forest of these evergreens: courtesy books such as *How to Make Friends with Girls, How to Speak in Public and Make Good Introductions, How to Become Rich and Avoid Poverty, How to Write Love Letters and Make Good Friendship with Girls, How to Know When a Girl Loves or Hates You, The Right Way to Approach Ladies and Get Them in Love*; moralistic manuals full of practical advice and warnings for the unwary, such as *Beware of Harlots and Many Friends, Never Trust All that Love You, What Women are Thinking about Men: No. 1 Bomb to Women, Life Turns Man Up and Down: Money and Girls Turn Man Up and Down*; political "histories" such as *Awolowo and Akintola in Political Crisis, Dr. Nkrumah in the Struggle for Freedom, The Struggles and Trials of Jomo Kenyatta, The Life Story and Death of John Kennedy*; novellas and plays such as *Rosemary and the Taxi Driver, Alice in the Romance of Love, Veronica My Daughter, The Game of Love: Classical Drama from West Africa*, and *Mabel the Sweet Honey that Poured Away*. These were books that appealed to both the head and heart. Like commercialized pulp classics in other cultures, they promised to instruct as well as entertain, giving the reader full value for his money, whatever his motives for buying. Indigenous publishers returning to the book trade in postwar Onitsha hoped to capitalize on what had proven popular and profitable previously.

Even the new pamphlets they produced after the war followed the old formulas. Writers returned to the same themes, same techniques, same stereotyped characters, and told basically the same hoary story in a new postwar setting; though the everyday world of these authors had changed radically, their art had not. The civil war was merely more grist for their mill, and they ground it pretty much the way they had pulverized previous material, reducing everything to crude pulp.

For example, shortly after the war numerous booklets tracing the course of events from the first military coup in 1966 to the Biafran surrender in 1970 began to appear in Ontisha bookstalls. Nearly every one of them had a picture of Major General Yakubu Gowon, Head of State and Commander in Chief of the Nigerian Armed Forces, on the cover and an author's disclaimer of authorship in the preface. J. Abiakam, who described himself as a "Poet, Historian, Actor, Novelist, Dramatist and Educationist," said in the introduction to *Important Records on Nigerian Civil War from 1966-1970* (Onithsa, n.d.) that "The statements in this book were actual statements made by those quoted, and dates mentioned were as a matter of truth the real days when the events took place" [sic] (p. 4). S. A. Rajih, in *The Complete Story of Nigeria Civil War for Unity (1966-1970) and Current Affairs* (Onitsha, 1971), wanted readers to know that his book "contains only verbal reports from Newspapers and Magazines. The Author did not add any word of his" (p. 3). A. N. Mba, in *The Story & Records of Nigerian Civil War for Unity 1966-1970 Including Current Affairs of the Twelve States Cabinet* (Onitsha, 1971), was even more emphatic: "May I inform readers that the contents of this book are mainly reports and publications from Magazines and Daily news papers. The author had not added any word of his own whatsoever" (p. 2). Such cautious prefatory remarks may be construed as attempts by the author/compiler to protect himself from charges of taking liberties with recent history – a potentially serious offence in a society that has just passed through a civil war – but prewar fact books on Lumumba, Kennedy, Nigerian independence, and other newsworthy personalities and events had contained similar prefaces. The postwar authors appear to have merely followed a tradition established by their predecessors who had compiled countless anthologies of this sort. Such booklets usually were devoid of overt political commentary.

It is tempting, of course, to hunt for covert political commentary in the postwar chapbooks and to interpret any deviations from the nonpartisan norm as residual Biafranisms. When one finds Wilfred Onwuka, a self-proclaimed "Historian, Poet, Actor, Author, Novelist and Dramatist," entitling his booklet *Selected Speeches of Odumegwu Ojukwu, General Gowon, Ukpabi Asika and Current Affairs* (Onitsha, n.d.), putting Ojukwu (the former secessionist leader) before Gowon (the Federalist leader) and then topping it off by placing a picture of Ojukwu on the cover, one suspects he has deliberately chosen to be very daring, perhaps even subversive, in his emphasis. However, the back cover of the same booklet carries a picture of Gowon and the title *Great Speeches of General Gowon, Odumegwu Ojukwu, Asika and Current Affairs of Nigeria*, and a quick glance at the contents shows that Ojukwu and Gowon are given almost exactly equal space, with Ukpabi Asika's brief speech throwing the balance of print to the Federalists. Author Onwuka – or perhaps his publisher – may have been carefully hedging his bets. One idly wonders if there is any significance in the fact that the booklet was published by the Survival Bookshop. In any case, the anthologist's art of making a diary of events out of scraps and snippets of news stories is a survival from earlier pamphleteering practice. There is nothing new about the organization of such booklets. The content may change from era to era but the form remains essentially the same.

More interesting are the works of fiction and drama written and published after the war, even though these too adhere to most of the old, established conventions. One extreme example of chapbook conservatism is Ikechukwu Okechukwu's *Veronica, The Girl: A True Account of a Thrilling Encounter between Love and Wealth* (Onitsha, n.d.), which was actually published in the "Republic of Biafra" during the war. It tells the hackneyed story of an educated girl who falls in love with a handsome young man and rejects a rich old chief who has won the support of her parents by promising to pay them an enormous bride price. The confrontation between the younger generation, represented by the girl and her boyfriend who insist on their right to marry for love, and the older generation, represented by the parents and the chief who still believe that parents have not only the right but the duty to arrange suitable matches for their children, is a stock situation in Onitsha market literature, having been popularized in such prewar bestsellers as *Veronica My Daughter, Elizabeth My Lover, True Love, Fineboy Joe and Beautiful Cathy, Agnes the Faithful Lover, Beautiful Maria in the Act of True Love, Alice in the Romance of Love, Miss Cordelia in the Romance of Destiny*, and *About Husband and Wife Who Hate Themselves*, to name just a few. One could say that the situation dramatizes the conflict between competing social codes in contemporary urban Africa: the Western-educated young people tend to opt for Western ways while their elders prefer to stick to indigenous customs and traditions. Okechukwu's handling of this theme does not differ much from that of his precursors. The girl eventually breaks with her family, runs off with the young man, and seems to be assured of a blissful life thereafter; unlike several other rebellious chapbook heroines,[6] she will suffer no hardships because her husband has a secure job as a bank teller in Onitsha. She has married for love but has not lost any money in the bargain. In Nigerian popular literature, there could be no happier ending.

What is most remarkable about this romantic melodrama is that the Nigerian civil war never enters into it. Indeed, the booklet appears to be the product of an earlier period of pamphlet writing, albeit published some time after the Biafran secession. Perhaps it was printed before shortages of paper, scarcity of presses and other ravages of war made chapbook publishing difficult. Or perhaps it was the kind of story that remained popular even during wartime. The entrapped Biafrans may have needed an escape literature.

The chapbooks produced after the war follow many of the earlier conventions but do not omit reference to the war. Indeed, some writers have used the war as a new backdrop or setting for a routine love story; others have focused on postwar problems, concentrating on the impact the war has had on the lives of some of its survivors. An example of the former is Grace Nnenna's *Love in the Battle Storm: A Story of War and Romance* (Enugu, n.d.), the back cover of which reads:

> Love in the Battle Storm is the story of an attractive nurse, Ifeoma Udozor who falls in love with a dashing young Orthopaedic Surgeon, Dr. Emeka Awa.
>
> A civil war breaks out in the country and Dr. Awa is posted to Santa Isabel to work with the Red Cross. During his absence Nurse Udozor meets Captain Afam Uzoma, an Officer of the rebel army. They get married, but their marriage is short-lived for Captain Uzoma is killed in the battle when Ifeoma was six months pregnant.
>
> Ifeoma is left to battle through the war and face the uncertainty of the future alone.

Actually, the book tells two separate love stories, the first of which – the relationship between nurse and doctor – proceeds without the slightest premonition of a civil war in the offing. It is not until the wedding invitations of the happy couple are being printed up that we hear for the first time of the Biafran secession. The subject is introduced abruptly and somewhat obliquely:

> Meantime there was mounting unrest in the country which eventually culminated into an open rebellion by some section of the population. The Government had to declare a State of emergency to stop the rebellion. (p. 50)

No political stand is taken on the war, and the author carefully avoids mentioning the names of any Nigerian or Biafran military leaders. The effect of the fighting on the nurse-heroine is immediate – she suddenly has much more work to do, gets separated from her fiance, and has to help her mother move to a new location – but she accepts these and other troubles stoically, regarding them as "unfortunate circumstances that confront one at one time or another in one's life." She never once blames her misfortunes on the Federalists or rebels. The only finger-pointing in the novel is done by some villagers suffering from dysentery who complain that "the white man and his civilization have brought this curse on us" (p. 56). Even the conclusion of the war is reported in neutral tones:

> The war came to a sudden and dramatic end. The rebels had surrendered.
> People received this dramatic end with mixed feelings. Many had lost their relations and belongings; many were homeless; while others had lost their jobs. (p. 75)

The message seems to be that war is hell for everybody, especially nurses, but no one is really responsible for it. The author of *Love in the Battle Storm* is more interested in examining the storm of love than the love battle.

Typical of another variety of postwar literature – the kind that exlores postwar problems – is Shakespeare C. N. Nwachukwu's *The Tragedy of Civilian Major* (Onitsha, 1972), which is summed up on its back cover as the story of a desperado:

> His real name was Uchenna Nweze...but people popularly knew him as "Civilian Major". He was an "attack" trader during the Biafra days. When the civil war ended, the abetted some soldiers who performed unfriendly acts against his town's people, and through this he made some money.
> When justice and order were established in his town, his ways of making money was sealed. [sic] He left for Kano, his prewar station and joined a gang of robbers. Later he seceeded [sic] from them in the hope of establishing his own gang in the East Central State. He planned to rest for some months at his town Ndiazi to enjoy his ill-gotten fortune, before proceeding to Onitsha where he chose as his would-be Headquarters.
> At home he ran in trouble with his people. The cup was full when he impregnated his kindred girl, Caroline, a class II student. The elders ordered him to cleanse the desecrated land. He refused and took them to court. It's an action-packed story, each page seems more exciting!

Armed robbery was a serious social problem in postwar Nigeria, and the story of 'Civilian Major' was undoubtedly intended to show what happened to young men who chose to live by the gun. Civilian Major makes lots of money working for a gang in northern Nigeria but when he returns home to the East to show off his wealth, which he claims to have earned as a trader in cloth, he immediately gets into serious trouble by seducing and impregnating a schoolgirl who turns out to be a distant relative. The leaders in the community try him in a native court, find him guilty and fine him heavily. He retaliates by suing the elders in the High Court, but loses his case. He plans to appeal the ruling, but before he has the opportunity, he is arrested at a roadblock and hauled off to prison for being in possession of a stolen car. After three days in prison, he writes his will, takes poison and dies. As the preface to the book points out, "The end of any avaricious criminal has never failed to be death, either by suicide or execution by the authorities. Thus the end of 'Civilian Major' spells out a distinct morale [sic] to the reader." (p. 3) In the popular imagination, the guilty are inevitably punished.

This narrative has many of the standard ingredients of Onitsha fiction – crime, sex, trials, imprisonment, suicide, a heavyhanded message at the end – all of which place it squarely in the mainstream of Nigerian popular writing. It merely extends the tradition of crime-does-not-pay literature to the postwar period. However, its attention to postwar problems makes it a new and timely contribution to the genre, one which to some extent reflects contemporary realities in Nigeria.

It is especially interesting to observe the author's depiction of the Federal troops who occupied the Igbo heartland after the war. The leaders of these troops are usually shown to be models of military discipline, decorum and decency, men who are genuinely committed to creating an atmosphere of trust and mutual respect. They try to win the confidence of the villagers and instill in the community a spirit of reconciliation, peace and harmony. When 'Civilian Major' attempts to persuade his old friend Corporal Musa to order some armed soldiers to arrest and torture the elders who have taken him to court, the Corporal adamantly refuses, saying:

> "How do you expect us to harass innocent men, men who had not broken the decrees of the Federal Military Government? We have a code of Conduct, I cannot go contrary to it, this is not the early stage of the end of the Civil war when anybody could act carelessly." (p. 47)

This corporal and his subordinates had not been so meticulous about army regulations earlier: "In some cases, they seezed [sic] bicycles, goats, and commandeered beautiful women, common characteristics of soldies [sic] all over the world when they are let loose" (p. 8). After one such seizure – the abduction of the daughter of 'Civilian major''s greatest enemy – the soldiers had to be taught their lesson: "When these careless actions became rampant people reported the offending troops to the Military policemen who took steps and punished them. And so order and peace reigned later" (p. 11). The message underscored here is that even for an occupying army, crime does not pay. Justice ultimately triumphs and the wicked are always punished. The postwar occupation of defeated Biafra has been reduced to the rigid logic of a chapbook formula.

These fictional narratives set in Igboland during and after the war and the factual anthologies mentioned earlier are not the only kinds of Onitsha market literature engendered by the war. There is yet another type which stands somewhere between fact and fiction. This is the pseudo-historical play based on real happenings but not pretending to be an accurate account of what actually occurred. One might call the genre legendary drama or theatre of the historically absurd. Before the war, many of these chapbook plays had been written about prominent African and non-African leaders: *The Last Days of Lumumba, Dr. Zik in the Battle for Freedom, Tshombe of Katanga, The Sorrows, Complete Treason and Last Appeal of Chief Awolowo and Others,* and *Sylvanus Olympio (The Assassinated President of Togo Republic): A Dramatic Story of the Man Who Laughed at Death* are but a few representative examples. Such plays spun legends out of the lives and deaths of famous men, often reinforcing and perpetuating myths about their attitudes and actions. It was perhaps inevitable that at least one should appear after the war called *The Last Days of Biafra* (Onitsha, 1972).

The author of this booklet, Orlando Thomas Iguh, explains in an introductory note that

> This drama "the last days of Biafra" represents the author's personal ideas of a few aspects of the numerous events which led to the emergence and collpase [sic] of the secessionist regime.
> The contents and names used therein are rather fictitious and have no bearing what so ever with any person living or dead. (p. ii)

The last statement is rather hard to accept, especially since at least one character, Major Nzeogwu, bears the same name as the Major whose role he enacts, and another, Military Governor Emeka, functions transparently in the role of Odumegwu-Emeka Ojukwu. Moreover, pictures of the real Nzeogwu and the real Ojukwu as well as of "His Excellency, Major General Gowon" adorn the cover and frontispiece of the booklet. There is no mistaking the leading men in this drama.

The play is really a piece of postwar anti-secessionist propaganda. Nearly every scene is set up as a debate, with the most admirable characters – particularly Major Nzeogwu – arguing the case against secession. Ojukwu is shown as being reluctant to bring war upon his people but feeling compelled by Federal actions to declare Biafra independent. He is encouraged to take a strong line by his advisers, his Consultative Assembly, and by Rivers chiefs who pledge their money and support to his cause. Ojukwu is portrayed not as a blackhearted villain but as a conscientious leader poorly advised – and perhaps the noblest Biafran of them all. It is clear the author thinks Ojukwu should have listened more attentively to

Nzeogwu, who courageously continues to speak out against secession even after Biafra has been created. Later, four Biafran military officers are tried and executed for treason, just as four were in the real Biafra. By the end of the war, even the common people are shown to be opposed to continuing the struggle for independence. One juju priest, praying to the gods of the land for peace, says:

> We now implore you once more to save us, our children and our women from the doom which a few young ones in our midst have unleashed upon our people...Initially we all supported Biafra. But after several months of fruitless and frightful fighting we no longer see any sense in fighting a senseless war.
>
> It is said that if the penis does not die young, it will surely eat bearded meat. It is in the hope that your young ones might live old enough to have an abundance of this meat of life, to reproduce and perpetuate the efforts of our forebears that we invoke you to put sense into the heads of our soldiers and their officers and halt this war immediately. (p. 43)

The play ends with Biafra's total surrender.

It is easy to dismiss such theatrics as inaccurate, farfetched, and wholly unreliable history, but the opinions expressed in the play may reflect authentic popular attitudes in contemporary Igboland toward the war and its leaders. What a given leader actually said and did during the war may be far less important to the common man than what that leader is believed to have said and done. The reputations of the best and worst men in history rest as much on hearsay as they do on hard evidence. The interpretation of Biafra's rise and fall offered in *The Last Days of Biafra* may therefore be a much closer reading of the mind of the average Federalist Igbo of this era – and in that sense, better history – than any textbook account could be.

However, it would be misleading to overemphasize the veracity of popular chapbook chronicles, fictional or otherwise. Some of them are sheer fabrications lacking the remotest resemblance to reality. As a horrible example, one can cite another postwar pamphlet entitled *The Complete Story and Trial of Adolf Hitler* (Onitsha, n.d.), which tells of the conflict between Hitler and "British War Prime Minister Mr. Wilson Churchill" who were "the brains behind the first and second World wars of 1914-1918 and 1939-1945" (p. 3). At one point Churc-Hill (the spelling of his name varies throughout the booklet) outlines his country's grievances against Hitler on BBC Radio:

> Six weeks ago, the German soldiers, navy and air force attacked Great Britain and damaged the government building in Liberia. Hitla's [sic] air force also bombed the civilian population of South Africa killing 9000 civilians, 40 innocent children and 60 pregnant women. At the same time, the German navy

with its sub-marine, opened fire at the British war ships and sunk 300 of them killing about 8000 British soldiers on board. Yesterday, Hitla's land force landed at Argentina – a Britain colony and committed rape, arson and genocide by wiping out all her inhabitants.

In Central Europe, the German air force bombed the British Cement Industry, killing the General Manager of the Industry and blastering the production machines into pieces and finally in America, it was reported that the German navy has blockaded the Northern Atlantic out of communication between America and India.

My government already has ordered the British soldiers out through his Majesty, King Judge the VI to arrest General Hitla and charge him before the Nation's National Court of Law. (pp. 12-13)

Hitler responds on German radio with counter-charges, including the assertion that

In the German Cameroons, Chuchill's rebels attacked the town of Yaunde from British Military base in the Northern part of South Africa, killing 2,000 men, 400 old men, 5,000 innocent children and His Royal Highness Chief Rago the III, the Kolonji of Yaunde. The aggressive soldiers destroyed the Roman Catholic Hospital, killing the medical officer in charge, 10 nursing sisters, 50 attendant nurses, 300 patients, 5 women in labour room, 21 newly born babies, 75 male staff of the hospital. (p. 14)

Hitler is finally captured and brought to trial in New York City, where he is defended by Jomo Kenyatta's famous barrister, Mr. Dingle Foot. He is acquitted on two charges but found guilty on the third – committing genocide against the Jews. Before a sentence can be handed down,

General Hitler broke the chains on his hands, jumped out of the dock and snatched a gun from one interpol. He shot the gun up and down the court. The court members, including the Judges took to their heels and ran for their lives. Then General Hitler disappeared. Nobody could tell Hitler's whereabouts up till today.

The End (p. 28)

Such creative historiography cautions us not to take Nigerian chapbook chronicles too literally.

Of course, one could argue that this bogus biography of Hitler, with its references to news broadcasts by heads of state, indiscriminate bombings of hospitals and other nonmilitary targets, vociferous denunciations of rebels and frequent accusations of genocide, actually reflects far more about the conduct of the Nigerian civil war than it does about the progress of any other wars. But this would make it no different from other "biographical" dramas produced in prewar Onitsha which also bent foreign history to conform to local expectations, knowledge and experience. Chapbook authors tend to be long on fancy when they are short of facts.

But we must also remember that these authors work according to the conventions of an established literary tradition, that they are hired craftsmen in a commercial industry, that they must write to sell. They cannot afford to waste their time with art for art's sake or history for history's sake. Their publishers are likely to be highly conservative, printing only what seems guaranteed of turning a quick profit. The market, with its inexorable laws of supply and demand, remains the final arbiter of literary tastes.

In postwar Nigeria a number of Onitsha publishers were willing to take risks on factual and fictional chapbooks dealing with the war, provided these were written according to tested and familiar formulas. The new blood-red wine had to be poured into the same bottles and purified of any lingering residues of Biafran spirits. Today the Onitsha literary marketplace appears to have returned to "business as usual." Apparently, it takes more than a civil war to change the habits of a veteran popular literature.

NOTES

1. For accounts of some of these writings, see Ernest Emenyonu, "Post-war Writing in Nigeria," *Studies in Black Literature*, 4, 1 (1973), 17-24; *Issue*, 3, 2 (1973), 49-54; *Ufahamu*, 4, 1 (1973), 77-92; and Anerobi Ngwube, "Nigerian war literature," *Indigo* (Lagos), 2 (1974), 3-4, 6-7.

2. Nigerian popular literature has been extensively studied. The best single source of information is Emmanuel Obiechina's *An African Popular Literature: A Study of Onitsha Market Pamphlets* (Cambridge: Cambridge UP, 1973), the introduction to which lists earlier scholarship.

3. Ulli Beier, "Public Opinion on Lovers: Popular Nigerian Literature Sold in Onitsha Market," *Black Orpheus*, 14 (1964), 4.

4. Don Dodson, "The Role of the Publisher in Onitsha Market Literature," *Research in African Literatures*, 4 (1973), 175.

5. Joseph C. Anafulu, "Onitsha Market Literature: Dead or Alive?" *Research in African Literatures*, 4 (1973), 166.

6. See, e.g., my "Nigerian Chapbook Heroines," *Journal of Popular Culture*, 2 (1968), 441-50.

The Rise of African Pornography

To the outside observer Africa has always been a surprising continent. "*Ex Africa semper aliquid novi*" (There is always something new from Africa) exclaimed Pliny the Elder nearly two thousand years ago, and his astonishment would be no less genuine if he were alive today. Even those who might be expected to know Africa fairly well through long experience or sound education – e. g., the explorers, missionaries, and colonial officials of yesteryear, the Peace Corps volunteers, veteran diplomats and academic Africanists of our time – have been known to express amazement upon learning of some new, bizarre phenomenon or event in what used to be called the Dark Continent. Whether this sharp shock of nonrecognition is the result of limited knowledge of the land and its peoples, of deeply-ingrained racial or cultural prejudices, of sheer inability to cope with the bewildering variety of life experiences possible in such a diversified environment, or whether it is the consequence of a combination of these and other factors is difficult to determine with any precision. It seems that no matter how enlightened the mind or liberated the spirit of the observer, Africa is bound at some point to defy his expectations, destroy his illusions, shatter his theories and wound his soul. And she will do this suddenly, unexpectedly, without advance warning. Africa is the most fickle of friends and a devastating enemy to easy generalizations.

One of the worst slurs Africa has had to endure from foreign observers is the notion that she was mute before she encountered Europe and merely inarticulate afterwards. It is assumed that she did not know how to sing until her colonial master taught her the music of his own language, thereby rescuing her from the ugly barbarism of her native tongues. Unfortunately, like Shakespeare's Caliban, she could be civilized only so far and no further, for she remained congenitally brutish and intractable, "a freckled whelp...not honoured with a human shape." What little eloquence she achieved was credited to the skill of Prospero, the master magician whose voice she purportedly sought to imitate in order to express her innermost feelings and ideas. Prospero had tried his best to recreate her in the image of Europe but he could not change her base nature entirely so she emerged from the imperial crucible imperfectly transformed and condemned to forever speak in a strange, inelegant accent. So, at least, read the histories of African literature written by Prospero's kith and kin, the loyal spokesmen for the colonizing culture.

It may be impossible to persuade such chroniclers to admit the validity of a different interpretation of Africa's literary development, especially one which places surprisingly heavy emphasis on the Africanness of African literature. The old arguments based on the integrity and beauty of African oral traditions and the pervasive influence these have had on African writing tend to fall on deaf ears, for the vigilant guardians of the Commonwealth of English letters have heard these arguments before, and knowing little about such traditions and even less about the nature of African languages, they usually choose to disregard them as unimportant or else dismiss their relationship to African written literature as unproven. In this paper, therefore, I will try a different approach and plead that African writing frequently stays resiliently African in spirit even when it becomes most transparently European in form, content and language. Caliban's triumph is to remain inextinguishably native, to speak in his own authentic voice despite all of Prospero's alchemy. To prove this, I intend to take an unhurried look at recent examples of African pornography, a form of cultural expression which, like venereal disease, undoubtedly spread to Africa through intimate contact with Europe.

The first specimen I wish to consider was called to my attention by a graduate student in my South African literature seminar last fall. He had come across it in a small supermarket in San Marcos, Texas, while hunting for fruits and nuts. Called *The Voortrekkers*,[1] it pretends to be a book written "more than one hundred years ago" by Jan de Villiers, a well educated Boer who "was among the courageous pioneers who travelled the Great Trek to the north" of South Africa in the mid-nineteenth century. An editor's preface to the First American Printing of this "complete and unexpurgated" Royal House Classic states that de Villiers worked on the manuscript "every day during the lonely nights of the trek...as a culturate [sic] form of entertainment" (p. 8) and that his text has been "untouched by any sort of editorial censorship" (p. 7). Even a few dozen Afrikaans words have been left untranslated, but the publisher thoughtfully supplies a four-page glossary at the end so the American reader won't miss a thing. As for the numerous four-letter words in the narrative, they are justified by the editors on the grounds that they provide necessary verbal verisimilitude:

> We believe that if we suppress – for the sake of a narrowminded sense of prudery – any of their deeply-felt expressions, their colorful terms, or their bold remarks which reflec [sic] so much the nature of their "human nature," we are also repressing the unadulterated manifestations of their true feelings and reactions under the stress of a nerve-wracking ordeal which they had voluntarily chosen to defy as the the sole means of survival available to them. The

utterances emanating from their anxiety, their rage, their sorrows, or their turbulent passions, bear a genuine image of the human soul, in the raw. (p. 7)

The first human soul we see in the raw is the heroine, Annie van Aards, who spends the opening chapter masturbating in a covered wagon. She is attracted to two men, a handsome but inexperienced youth ludicrously named Christiaan, and his father Johannes, the supermasculine leader of the wagon train. Her problem is stated in tactful metphor: "Did the filly mate with the untried colt? Or with the stallion, scarred by a hundred battles?" (p. 11). Annie's solution is to sample both before making a decision on a more permanent liaison.

There are plenty of oversexed minor characters in the novel, too, so the action never flags and every chapter contains at least one muscularly detailed account of an outstanding orgasm. The diversity of erotic interactions is impressive; besides varying the positions and partners of the principal fornicators, the author introduces episodes involving cunnilingus, fellatio and homosexual anal intercourse. When there are no more nooks or crevices left to explore, the story moves to a rather conventional climax with the heroine choosing the younger man, riding off to meet him at a deserted spot, and there being gang-raped by a howling horde of Kaffir warriors whose enormous ebony members tear her apart. She is literally done in at the end and left for the circling vultures.

Lest my motives for summarizing the highlights of *The Voortrekkers* be misunderstood, I should like to make it perfectly clear that I do not consider this book to be African pornography. Pornography it is, but African it certainly is not. I insist it is unAfrican not because the author is white (though this would be reason enough) but because the book does not provide an African perspective on sexual experience, real or imaginary. *The Voortrekkers* is nothing but Western pornography set in Africa. It addresses Western readers, embodies Western attitudes and beliefs, and appeals to Western prurient interests which may be totally different from African prurient interests.

Besides all this, the book is an obvious fraud. The modern American idiom in which it is written gives it sway. Would a Boer writing in the mid-nineteenth century have his characters say things like:

"Come and get it, Lover." (p. 93)
"I don't want to see your miserable face again, do you hear me? Get lost!" (p. 111) "Cheap slut!...I'm gonna fuck the hell out of you! I'm gonna screw you, like nobody has!" (p. 144)
"Oh, he was fucking her real good, real good." (p. 151)
"Who is that creep whom you allowed to deflower you, you shamelesss hussy!" (p. 156)

Even if the bona fide Americanness of one or two of these quotations can be questioned, there are enough references to pistons, steel lacework, neurotic insecurity, pathological fear, limbo dancers, he-men, luscious blonds and lousy shits to identify the narrative style as foreign to Victorian South Africa. It is of course conceivable that the book was actually based on an unpublished manuscript by a white South African – possibly even a voortrekker – but if so, the American editors of Royal House Classics evidently took great liberties with the raw material they dug up. They appear to be quite conscious of the stylistic inconsistencies in the novel for they are careful to state in the preface that

> Although the author was a learned man, whose formal education was acquired within the solemn chambers of Eton, Oxford and Cambridge, it is evident that, under the obvious stress of the immense journey, his speech suffered a logical transformation under the influence of the others, who were not as fortunate as he was and had little or no education at all. (p. 8)

But this is taking us away from the central point. *The Voortrekkers* is clearly an example of run-of-the-mill Western pornography which strives to be different by setting commonplace characters into lascivious motion in an unusual time and place. It is nothing more than a variation on the familiar American pioneer theme, with the Kaffirs of the High Veld substituting for the Injuns of the Great Plains. Published in a new international series by an established American under-the-counter press, it appears to be aimed at those jaded pornophiles who like a little exoticism with their eroticism. It is interesting to us only as an imaginative projection, a phallic fantasy, a voyeur's voyage into the groin of Africa via the lubricious daydreams generated by the perverted muse of the Western world.

A more genuine example of African pornography is a paperback recently published by Di Nigro Press in Nigeria under the provocative title *Sex is a Nigger.*[2] Written by Naiwu Osahon, a prolific new author educated at business colleges in England, it tells of the amorous exploits of a lusty young Nigerian student on holiday in Scandinavia. Much of the book is a private travelogue with Henry, the seasoned playboy hero, serving as explorer and tour guide through the feminine wonders of the Nordic world. Needless to say, he is adored by every woman he meets, and he leaps from one to the next with extraordinary equestrian ease. His only problem is to detach himself long enough from Sonja, his Swedish steady, and Grethe, his Danish tart, to make regular contacts with Birgitta, Kerstin, Gunila, Eva, Inger, Birgit, Barbro, Diana and any others who might cross his unbridled path. He finally gets a timetable worked out so he can make the rounds efficiently and meet all his bedroom obligations without strain. At the end, he is rather relieved that his holiday in Scandinavia is over because some of his girlfriends are beginning to cling too close and he wants to shed them all and start afresh in England.

As can be seen from this brief summary, the novel is less an ethnography of Scandinavian sexual behavior than it is a black crow of masculine triumph in a white world. The hero is never rebuffed, never refused, never repulsed, never rejected; Henry the Great merely has to wave his sizable magic wand and he conquers all. His adventures may therefore serve the same function for African readers that the hypereroticism in *The Voortrekkers* does for Western readers. Both books appeal to very basic human psycho-sexual needs and desires, for in this kind of pornography there are no personal inadequacies, no moral hang-ups, no permanent frustrations, no unattainable delights, nothing to interfere with total gratification and complete indulgence in sensually pleasurable activities. All the usual barriers are down, and everything, even the impossible, is suddenly, fantastically possible.

What makes *Sex is a Nigger* different from Western pornography in general and *The Voortrekkers* in particular is the attitude it expresses toward sex. In *Sex is a Nigger* extreme sexual behavior is treated humorously; in *The Voortrekkers* it is a very serious business indeed. The Nigerian author distances his reader from the sexual act by laughing at it, while the Western author tries to bring his reader close to the experience by immersing him in every slippery physiological detail. Both set their stories in faraway lands where sexual fantasies can be given freer rein, unchecked by impinging local realities, but their motives for writing appear to be fundamentally different; whereas the African pornographer seeks primarily to entertain, his European or American counterpart seeks most earnestly to arouse. African pornography is romantic comedy; Western pornography is biological melodrama.

A few examples may help to illustrate the difference. Here are some typical erotic episodes from *Sex is a Nigger*. In the first, Henry's new-found Danish girlfriend Grethe helps him recover from a bout of seasickness on the boat to Sweden.

> She tried sharing the narrow bed with me, but she fell off and I told her to come on top as she wouldn't fall from that position. She tried my suggestion. She was on top of me face to face and my dizziness seemed to stop.
> "You know you have cured my dizziness?" I said as I unzipped my pants and pulled them down.
> "Have I?" she asked, allowing me to pull up her skirt.
> "Yes, you have," I said, hauling down her flimsy knickers.

"Then I will stay here until it's time to get out of the ship," she said jokingly, her flesh now pressed on mine.

"That is exactly what I would love you to do!" I gasped and held her tightly and kissed her passionately. I tried penetrating her and she spread her legs to encourage me. I went right in and could hear her panting. She reached her peak early even before I did, then she held me close and kissed me still more sweetly. We rolled over, so that I was now on top and went on and on in a series of atomic bursts. (p. 41)

Henry's megaton virility is later tested and found pleasurably annihilating by Eva:

We began slowly, if you know what I mean. There was no need to hurry, for we had all the night before us, and the end, we knew, would be more exhausting than the Zulu war.

At first the squeaking bed was music to us, but we soon lost our sense in each other as we built up momentum, then came the first of a fierce war of charges and countercharges. At each climax she was crying, "you are very sweet...you are too sweet!...you are wonderful, wonderful, wonderful!" There were a lot of incomprehensible phrases, but I was too involved, and I could only guess they were all complimentary.

At such rare moments of high passion, nothing is taken down in evidence against anyone. (pp. 121-22)

A few pages later Henry is involved with two girls at once:

At about 3 a.m. they suggested we go to bed, and without any ceremony they stripped naked, then, as if planned, they rushed to kiss me on both cheeks and offered to help me undress. Before I could protest, my trousers were down. It is not often that one meets two pretty and stark naked girls offering to undress you, so I obliged them.

Just below my waist I was already weighing more than normal. They could see "it", feel "it", play with "it". I was so tickled I made a mess of their carpet. Then the three of us together jumped into the bed and their full naked length was rubbing close against my very warm sides, giving me instant electric shocks and inducing me to give one of them at a time a lion's share of my more active side. Somehow I made sure they both had a fair share of my essence, and neither had any reason to be jealous of the other. (p. 125)

Henry's most idyllic erotic experience occurs on the beach with Barbro, a girl who peels off her colthes as soon as they are alone together:

There she was, a silent naked goddess. Her tan scintillating in the burning light, her hands, spread open to embrace, her eyes wet in anticipation of love.

Stripping off my pants, I pounced on my goddess like an elephant, hungry for sex. My weight was overbearing, my eagerness at its height, her willingness complete. We reeled and reeled on the sand, locked tight by the waists. There was no fear of outside interruption. It was a quiet, secluded spot and we were doing our best not to violate the peace.

It was a different experience in the sun. Perhaps that was how Nature had intended things to be. I was jerking powerfully non-stop, like a factory machine, and she was responding to my rhythm.

The sun was beating hot on my back, melting perspiration to reduce my rising temperature. Her own perspiration was washing with mine to soak us and the sandy beach. The sudden burst of ejaculation was uncontrollable, and for once, I feared I might have made a girl pregnant. It was a wonder I hadn't already, of course, having pumped so much much into so many, but I had always relied on their taking precautions. (pp. 141-42)

Henry's amusing asides to the reader, his unabashed enthusiasm for bawdy gymnastics, his tendency toward hyperbole in describing his delights, and his extravagant animal, mechanical and military imagery reveal a carefree comic attitude toward sex. For Henry, fucking is great fun, and part of the pleasure is in the telling of it. He revels in the word as well as the deed and often creates humor by translating the urgent impulses of the flesh into incongruously nonchalant comments on his conquests. He is a happy-go-lucky libertine.

In *The Voortrekkers*, on the other hand, the leading characters are bestial, and their idiom of intercourse is fury and rage. Lovers assault one another cruelly, purging their passions in rough, brutal, carnal combat. They thrill to violating and being violated, and achieve ecstasy only through mutual masochism. One or two examples will suffice:

He glared at her, a tigerish gleam in his eyes, grabbed her by the hair and threw her down on the kaross. "You witch, you want it, and now I'm going to give it to you – my way. I'm going to fuck the hell out of you. I'll rip your cunt apart with my cock, you hear me? I'm gonna have you, you witch..."

He lowered himself on her as she spread for his entrance. He thrust himself into her, pumping away, ignoring her whimpering, pushing deeper into the narrow channel of flesh.

He was tearing her apart. Again, she felt searing pain so intense, it became devastating pleasure. Finally, she joined into his passionate rhythm and she moved beneath him, accommodating him, her legs about his thighs ...

Annie was rolling her head on the kaross, moaning and groaning wildly as Christiaan increased the tempo of his lunges. I won't let myself go, she thought dimly, but even while thinking it, she was swooning, all bathed in the lubricating fluid of her final spasm. (pp. 95-98)

In another lusty scene, pain and pleasure are similarly intermingled:

> She gasped painfully as he shoved it forward, ramming it completely inside her hot lubricated passage. His prick encased in the warm clasping sheath pulsated with lewd pleasure. He wanted to hurt her, to make her bleed; it was a wild desire in him to which he couldn't resist. He went pushing his cock slightly deeper then withdrawing it completely. Then the heavy weight of his loins crashed hard against her crotch, and Johannes' long thick cock slithered into her hot throbbing passage.
>
> "Aaaaaagggggh!" she strangled through clenched teeth. Her vaginal passage was on fire. The great thick phallus penetrating it at such speed and with great strength felt like a drill tunneling deep into her belly, pulling as under the walls of her tender vagina. A searing pain and warm sensation of running blood tore through her loins. Annie struggled and swung her buttocks in vain to escape the cruel impalement. It was no use. Johannes had skewered into her up to the hilt, she was stuck on his rockhard cock. Her lips opened and closed in torment as she felt her cunt walls afire from the unaccustomed size of the instrument driving in her belly. But the ravishment was also sending unfamiliar thrills of wicked pleasure coursing through her entire being. She began to undulate her hips lasciviously in rhythm to the long thick cock fucking into her cunt with such energy.
>
> "Oh, God," she gasped, "I like it, I like it, go on..." (pp. 149-50)

Psychoanalysts have commented on a "fascinating paradox at the root of pornography":

> Overtly it is militantly devoted to describing states of ecstatic sensuality and abandonment to mutual orgiastic pleasure. But all that it actualizes is an orgiastic expertise in the physical manipulation of the own body-self and the *other's* bodily organs. Hence a certain manic quality, which infests the narrative.[3]

This manic quality is present in *The Voortrekkers* but absent from *Sex is a Nigger*, which is a much milder form of pornography because it expresses a happy hedonism instead of an all-consuming psychosomatic rage. The characters in the Nigerian novel do not attempt to subjugate, injure or humiliate one another sexually. They are content to savor life's earthy pleasures to the full, and they don't require bitterness to give sharper flavor to what they recognize as deliciously sweet. In Western pornography, sex must hurt in order to bring about voluptuous fulfillment, but in African pornography, sex invariably tickles.

These sweeping generalizations can easily be overturned if we can find but one example of Western pornography which manifests all or most of the characteristics identified herein as African. I'm sure there are many excellent specimens to choose from. Terry Southern and Mason Hoffenberg's *Candy* might be an obvious choice since its approach to sex tends to fall on the side of humorous relish rather than obsessional spice. But *Candy* and books like it are really parodies of Western pornography which gain much of their comic strength from their deliberate deviation from the accepted norm. Though Susan Sontag, in her essay on "The Pornographic Imagination," insists that *"Candy* may be funny, but it's still pornography" because it prefers ready-made conventions of character, setting, and action,[4] I think it's legitimate to draw a distinction between hard-core pornography and "meta-pornography," which serves as a humorous reflection of and comment on the salient characteristics of the genre.

However, perhaps for our purposes it would be more helpful to formally define the differences between hard-core and soft-core pornography, since our African example seems to fall into the latter category, being neither meta-pornography nor rigidly hard-core. But formal discriminations are very difficult to make. If we were to accept Masud R. Khan's assertion that hard-core pornography "is largely, if not exclusively, used for masturbation"[5] and to assume that soft-core pornography is not, we would then have no other recourse than to take an official poll of all available masturbators. ("Would those in favor, *please* raise their hands?") Perhaps it is sufficient to say that African pornography is different from Western pornography and to leave it at that.

But a more serious objection may be raised. We have examined only one example of African pornography and we are basing all our statements on that one text. Is there additional evidence to present before the jury or does the case rest here? The truth of the matter is that pornographic books written in European languages by African authors are extremely rare, and they may not exist at all in any African vernaculars. The reasons for this are fairly clear. Until quite recently, Africa has not had many publishing houses of its own, and African authors have had to either send their manuscripts abroad to European or American publishers or else submit them to the few local missionary or government presses that were in the business of producing books for school use in Africa. It is rather unlikely that missionaries or government officials would have been eager to publish a book like *Sex is a Nigger* and disseminate it in the schools. European and American publishers probably wouldn't have touched it either, unless it were written in best-seller prose or stood a chance of winning an international prize as "the first African novel to tell the whole truth about black Africa after dark." The aspiring African pornographer simply didn't have an opportunity to market his wares until small publishing houses catering to the reading interests of the average man began to spring up in Africa.

One place they did so in profusion was southern Nigeria, where mass literacy campaigns, rapid expansion of the educational system, and the availability of printing presses after the Second World War conspired to provide both the market and the means necessary for a viable local publishing industry. The prolific output of these popular presses, which tended to specialize in inexpensive educational, political or literary pamphlets, cannot be described in detail here,[6] but their contribution to the rise of African pornography merits a few paragraphs.

First, let it be stated loud and clear that they produced no hard-core pornography. Whether this is because there was no interest in this kind of literature in Nigeria, or no one to write it, or no publisher willing to risk printing it, is unknown. It is entirely possible that Africans don't respond to the crude Manichean manner in which sexual business is transacted in Western drugstore classics. It is also conceivable that they respond better to their own brand of randy bluntness, a brand which includes hilarity as a seminal ingredient. The literary chapbooks published in Onitsha, the hub of popular publishing in Nigeria, frequently contain frank but funny accounts of energetic copulation. Here is one from *Rosemary and the Taxi Driver*, an Onitsha best-seller:

> They rocked each other, hugging themselves together, feeling the transfer flirtation and fervourism, through the sending over, of the warmth, which God had wasted time, in giving over to any living belong, excepting the reptiles. Their intentions were deep, mostly that of Okoro. His sexual instinct was in its worst intensive urgent. Startled were the leaves around, mourning under the roary wind. The scaring desert winded over with tremor. They like doing the lot, the life they played was as the first day of a virgin in a honeymoon. How beautiful it is for Rosemary to feel very shy and sophisticated. Her youthful fidelity was exhausted and they delved into romantic blast.[7]

Now here is an episode from *Mabel the Sweet Honey that Poured Away*, written by an author who calls himself Speedy Eric:

> He put his lips squarely on her neck just below the chin and sucked avariciously. That was not enough. He opened two buttons on her blouse exposing her conical breasts. He placed his lips just at the tip of the thing and began to suck. In fact the girl began to quiver all her body began to dance frantically. She threw her arms on his neck and held him down to her tight. At the same time their waists were making marvellous gestures.
>
> After that he raised his lips to her own lips and kissed her so strong that she screamed without knowing. Yet her arms had gone round Gil's waist holding him down to her trembling body. Her legs were kicking wildly with excitement.
>
> It was terrific. Mabel forgot her entire self. She gave up her entire self. Her eyes were closed. She was breathing fast. And Gil? I wish my brains were good enough to allow me give you a full and fitting description of his wildness. His

entire frame was dancing like a jelly-fish; to see his eyes, you would swear that he had been drinking alcoholics for the past four hours.[8]

I think perhaps my point is made, but let me reiterate it just once more for emphasis. African pornography, though similar to and no doubt genetically descended from its precursors in Europe and America, manifests a much more playful attitude toward sex than does hard-core Western pornography. African pornographic heroes and heroines appear to be able to accept the simple sensual pleasures of life with joy and enthusiasm; they do not have to mutilate their lovers or agonize over their ecstasies. But they do like to talk about their fleshly adventures, elaborating on them with zesty exaggeration and zany detail. They are not pathologically obsessed with sex but delightfully addicted to it. In other words, they are African, not European or American.

The Africanness of African pornography (and of any other species of African literature, for that matter) resides in its soul rather than in its external trappings. African writers may have adopted Western forms, techniques, and languages to express themselves, but the selves they express remain inerasably African. They adapt whatever they adopt to suit their own psyches, creating something unique for themselves out of what had been held in common by others. The result, as we have seen, has been the emergence of a literature which is genuinely African and not merely an illegitimate offspring of Western literary tradition. If this comes as news to anyone, I wouldn't be surprised.

NOTES

1. Jan de Villiers, *The Voortrekkers* (n.p.: Royal House Classic, 1968). All quotations are taken from this edition.

2. Naiwu Osahon, *Sex is a Nigger* (Lagos: Di Nigro Press, 1971). All quotations are taken from this edition.

3. Masud R. Khan, "The Abuses of Literacy – 4: The Politics of Subversion and Rage," *Times Literary Supplement*, 4 February, 1972, p. 121.

4. Susan Sontag, *Style of Radical Will* (New York: Dell, 1966), p. 51.

5. Khan, p. 122.

6. The best single source of information on this literature is Emmanuel Obiechina, *An African Popular Literature: A Study of Onitsha Market Pamphlets* (Cambridge: Cambridge UP, 1973). Other useful introductory studies are Donatus Nwoga, "Onitsha Market Literature," *Transition*, 19 (1964), 26-33; Ulli Beier, "Public Opinion on Lovers: Popular Nigerian Literature Sold in Onitsha Market," *Black Orpheus*, 14 (February 1964), 4-16; and Nancy J. Schmidt, "Nigeria: Fiction for the Average Man," *Africa Report*, 10, 8 (August 1965), 39-41.

7. Miller O. Albert, *Rosemary and the Taxi Driver* (Onitsha: Chinyelu Printing Press, n.d.), p. 29. All spelling and punctuation errors have been preserved.

8. Speedy Eric, *Mabel the Sweet Honey that Poured Away* (Onitsha: A Onwudiwe & Sons, n.d.), p. 39. All spelling and punctuation errors have been preserved.

Popular Literature in East Africa

Twenty-five years ago, at the beginning of the era of independence, East Africa was considered a literary desert. Although there was a trickle of activity in Kiswahili, Luganda, Acoli and a few other African languages – a trickle partly induced by the need for reading matter in these languages in East African primary schools – there was virtually nothing being written by East African authors in English, the colonial tongue that had become the national language of Uganda, Kenya and Tanganyika (now Tanzania). While vigorous African literary movements in English had already been set in motion in South Africa and in parts of West Africa, East Africa was conspicuous for its failure to produce a single writer or even a single literary work of any significance. Barren, sterile, silent, uncreative, dead – these were the adjectives applied in those days to the East African literary scene.

The situation was an embarrassment to East Africans who were called upon to explain this curious deficiency. Taban lo Liyong recalls the humiliation he experienced when invited to speak to a group at Howard University:

> I was to talk about the literary climate in my country: East Africa. As you well know, we do not have much to show. I cleared my voice and assumed the seriousness of a professor emeritus...I said we have a very authoritative anthropological work on the Gikuyu tribe; Mau Mau reminiscences; a few political works elaborating the concept called African Socialism; some political complaints, a few tales and...I halted. There were shufflings of feet on the wooden floor. Somebody cleared his throat. "Literature man, tell us about literature." I mentioned the name Rebeca Njau. They asked what she has written. I could not remember. I told them of Grace Ogot. Certainly they have read her stories in Rajat Neogy's *Transition*. Some said yes, some no. I told them off. I am not responsible for their ignorance...I got disgusted. I stood up to walk out. The fact is, all in all, I had contributed nothing.
>
> I walked to my apartment, threw my bookcase on the bed and sat next to it. I then held my big head between my powerful hands. I squeezed it, and squeezed it hard, till it thought. When thoughts came, they poured like tropical rain: big and fast. I pulled out a pencil and a paper and wrote fast, capturing every drop of thought.[1]

Taban wasn't the only one to squeeze his head between his hands and wring out some inspiration. A great many East Africans began writing creatively in

47

English in the mid and late Sixties, and an even greater number managed to achieve publication in the Seventies. Indeed, if one were to measure literary movements in terms of quantity of production, East Africa would probably lead the continent in prolificity (though some critics might prefer to term it profligacy). Certainly East Africa seems to have generated the movement with the most momentum today. The desert is now in spectacular bloom.

The first sign of incipient literary life appeared in 1964 when Heinemann's new African Writers Series published *Weep Not, Child*, a *Bildungsroman* set in the Mau Mau era, which had been written by a Gikuyu undergraduate named James Ngugi (now known as Ngugi wa Thiong'o). Another novel by Ngugi, *The River Between*, also concerned with documenting a particular interval in Gikuyu history during the colonial period, appeared the following year, and Ngugi's longest and richest novel, *A Grain of Wheat*, describing the aftermath of the struggle for independence, was published in 1967. Thus, almost by default, Ngugi became the first serious writer of English expression to emerge in East Africa, and his attempts to reconstruct in fiction the history of his own people under colonial rule – a task that Chinua Achebe had undertaken with great success in West Africa only a few years earlier – set a precedent which a number of other young East African writers elected to follow. Ngugi was not only his country's first important novelist but also the founding father of a school of East African writing concerned with revaluating the African past.

The next serious writer of any consequence to emerge in East Africa was a comedian, Okot p'Bitek of Uganda, whose satirical *Song of Lawino*, published in 1966 by the newly established East African Publishing House after being rejected by several European publishers, took East Africa by storm. It was the first locally published literary work in English to achieve widespread popularity, and its impact on subsequent East African writing was immediate and profound. *Song of Lawino* is a long poem, purportedly a lament, sung by an uneducated woman who has lost the affection of her educated husband. She complains that her husband, who once wooed and loved her, now insults and despises her because she is illiterate and ignorant of Western ways. He is infatuated with all things modern and unAfrican and has recently taken up with a young woman in the city who wears such symbols of progress as lipstick, a wig and a padded brassiere. Here is a sample of Lawino's description of her rival:

> Her lips are red hot
> Like glowing charcoal,
> She resembles the wild cat
> That has dipped its mouth in blood,
> Her mouth is like raw yaws

It looks like an open ulcer,
Like the mouth of a fiend!
Tina dusts powder on her face
And it looks so pale;
She resembles the wizard
Getting ready for the midnight dance;

She dusts the ash-dirt all over her face
And when little sweat
Begins to appear on her body
She looks like the guinea fowl!
.... ..
Some medicine has eaten up Tina's face;
The skin on her face is gone
And it is all raw and red,
The face of the beautiful one
Is tender like the skin of a newly born baby!

And she believes
That this is beautiful
Because it resembles the face of a white woman!
Her body resembles
The ugly coat of the hyena;
Her neck and arms
Have real human skins!
She looks as if she has been struck
By lightning;
Or burnt like the kongoni
In a fire hunt.

And her lips look like bleeding,
Her hair is long,
Her head is huge like that of the owl,
She looks like a witch,
Like someone who has lost her head
And should be taken
To the clan shrine!
Her neck is rope-like,
Thin, long and skinny
And her face sickly pale.[2]

Lawino's "lament" is actually an attack on the Westernization of Africa, with her husband Ocol and his girlfriend Tina serving as synecdoches for the moral and cultural confusion that has afflicted many educated Africans. The attack is entertaining in form and style but discomfiting in effect. p'Bitek manages to tickle and sting at the same time. It was this kind of satirical hilarity with very sober undertones that p'Bitek introduced into East African writing with *Song of Lawino*. He went on to compose *Song of Ocol* (1970) (the husband's answer to Lawino), *Song of Prisoner* and *Song of Malaya* (both published as *Two Songs* in 1971) in essentially the same idiom, and then turned his hand to *Song of Soldier*, which treats a more contemporary political theme with characteristic laughter mixed with tears. p'Bitek had mastered the art of serving up bitter social criticism with a smile.

The next writer to make an impression on the East African literary scene was Charles Mangua, whose racy first novel *Son of Woman* was published in 1971. *Son of Woman* is a picareque tale of the adventures of Dodge Kiunyu, the son of a prostitute who is left to fend for himself at an early age and gets into many scrapes and entanglements in his slippery passage through life. The East African Publishing House blurb on the back cover of the novel calls the story a

> morality, ushering us into an underworld of sex, violence and corruption. Stripping his soul bare, and telling it like it is, [Dodge Kiunyu] reveals weaknesses of character that are universal, the big and little foibles that make life bearable. We see him as an orphan in the shanties of Nairobi; as a young man frequenting houses of ill-repute for a "tumble"; as a Makerere student, a corrupt civil servant and finally, a seasoned jailbird.

Another way of putting it would be to say that the novel is little more than a loose, episodic narrative of a rake's progress written in a jazzy, colloquial style. The central character, a self-confessed opportunist who tries through trickery and deceit to move ever upward in a chaotic world, enlists our sympathy only because he frequently fails in his contorted efforts due to a fatal and somewhat comical weakness for voluptuous women. He lives by his wits but gets trapped by his gonads. He is an overreacher with a phallic flaw.

Yet it would be an injustice to Charles Mangua to dismiss *Son of Woman* as an inconsequential potboiler. Potboiler it may be, but inconsequential it certainly has not been, at least not in East Africa. This novel has probably done more than any other book to loosen up the literary climate of East Africa and pave the way for the rise of an indigenous popular literature. Other writers – including Ugandans such as Okello Oculi in his novel *Prostitute* (1968) and even Okot p'Bitek in his poems *Song of Prisoner* and *Song of Malaya* – had treated the seamy side of life in a distinctive personal style, but no one had made a big commerical success of it until Mangua came along and turned sidewalk tragedy into gutter comedy.

Suddenly publishers woke up to the fact that there was money to be made in such books, and there has been a rash – indeed, a growing pox – of similar publications issued in recent years. Publishers, in trying to cater to the reading interests of the public and capitalize on the most popular fads, have themselves helped to catapult faint tendencies into firm trends by trying to repeat their greatest successes. So many literary works have been published in Nairobi lately that it is becoming increasingly difficult to track them all down and sort them all out into logical categories, but it is clear that several of the most prominent themes are being reworked today to suit the popular temper. The kind of deflation of literary value that is apparent in the gradual progression from Ngugi's serious historical fiction of the early Sixties to p'Bitek's amusing satirical poetry of the late Sixties to Mangua's frivolous proletarian potboilers of the early Seventies is now being duplicated in every genre as imitators with far less talent flood the market with their insipid drivel. In such circumstances one begins to ask a little nervously if there is an immutable law of supply and demand that causes bad literature to drive out good. Will East Africa's best literary impulses be drowned in a swamp of pulp?

Before getting too alarmed about this prospect, let us look at the evidence of change. First, the Ngugi school, possibly the most stable of the three discussed so far. A few years after Ngugi's earliest works appeared, Grace Ogot published *The Promised Land* (1966), a historical novel describing the unsuccessful migration of a Kenya Luo family to unoccupied farmland in Tanganyika, and Khadhambi Asalache, another Kenyan writer, told the story of a struggle for chieftainship in a precolonial Kenyan village in *A Calabash of Life* (1967). These attempts at historical reconstruction dealt with peoples other than the Gikuyu, but soon such works as Leonard Kibera's stories in *Potent Ash* (1967?), Godwin Wachira's *Ordeal in the Forest* (1968), Charity Waciuma's *Daughter of Mumbi* (1969), John Karoki's *The Land is Ours* (1970) and Stephen N. Ngubiah's *A Curse from God* (1970) returned attention to the disruption of Gikuyu life during the Mau Mau era. This was a nationalist literature for it was concerned with reinterpreting the past from an East African perspective and particularly with reappraising the crucial role in Kenya's history played by the Mau Mau rebels, who were now seen as heroic freedom fighters instead of atavistic terrorists. In the mid-1970s this patriotic literary trend continued in such works as Kenneth Watene's plays *My Son for My Freedom* (1973) and *Dedan Kimathi* (1974), Meja Mwangi's novels *Carcase for Hounds* (1974) and *Taste of Death* (1975), and Ngugi wa Thiong'o and Micere Githae-Mugo's new play *The Trial of Dedan Kimathi* (1977), all of which dealt with aspects of the armed struggle during the Emergency period.

By the early Seventies the Mau Mau uprising had become such a well-worn literary theme in Kenya that at least one writer tried to give it a new twist. This was Charles Mangua, who built his second episodic novel, *A Tail in the Mouth* (1972), around the adventures of a picaresque hero who becomes involved in the Emergency, first as a home guard and later as a freedom fighter. The attitude toward the Mau Mau expressed in this jumbled tale is ambivalent. A few of the freedom fighters are depicted as heroic but most are crude and vulgar cutthroats with no redeeming qualities. Mangua's purpose seems to be to debunk historical mythmaking, just as he debunks organized religion, village administration, the legal system, and life in the metropolis by making his hero alternately a seminarian, a land owner, an accused murderer, a taxi driver and a drunkard. Even though Mangua touches on some serious issues in all this confusion, it is difficult to take *A Tail in the Mouth* seriously as a criticism of society. Because the story lacks a coherent moral center, it reads more like a popular travesty than a politcal tract. Certainly nothing patriotic appears to have been intended by the author. Mau Mau was simply another target for Mangua's gleeful irreverence and cynicism.

The p'Bitek school of satirical song has suffered a similar deterioration of artistic and ethical standards in recent years. The success of p'Bitek's experiments in composing verse soliloquies encouraged many others to attempt to express their social ideas in similar form. First Okello Oculi wrote *Orphan* (1968), an interesting long poem he termed a "village opera" because it employed a number of different speakers in a community reflecting on a number of related private and public concerns. Then Joseph Buruga brought out *The Abandoned Hut* (1969), a pale imitation of *Song of Lawino* in which an uneducated man attacks the foibles of an educated woman. Both of these long poems appear to have been inspired by p'Bitek's pioneering work.

The next important verse soliloquy to appear in East Africa was David Maillu's *My Dear Bottle* (1973), a dissipated man's apostrophe to the instrument of his dissipation. Maillu followed this up with *After 4:30* (1974), a prostitute's complaint about the insatiable sex drives of bosses and bureacrats who have female employees at their mercy and frequently force them into prostitution. Then Maillu composed a three-volume poem called *The Kommon Man* (1975, 1976) which covers the private and public life of an average man immersed in greater-than-average difficulties. This 850-page poem, certainly the longest to have been written in English by an African writer, provides a panoramic view of East African society from the perspective of an insider, someone caught in the maelstrom of forces that shape the lives of working-class people in a modern African city. Themes such as marital infidelity, official corruption, bureaucratic inefficiencies, political opportunism and money madness are woven through this long song of domestic discord like obsessive refrains to which the singer returns again and again. There is no reluctance to speak frankly and forthrightly about the exploitation of the poor by the rich, an exploitation that often takes physical form. Here is the opening of the first chapter, which is entitled, "My Wife's Legs":

> He who hides his disease
> cannot expect to be cured.
> Though they say
> domestic affairs are not talked about
> in the public square,
> it takes two to make a quarrel, but
> it might take the whole public square
> to settle the damage of the quarrel.
>
> The dog I bought now bites me, and
> the fire I kindled now burns me.
> They say
> if you dig too deep for fish
> you may come up with a snake...
> I say
> I dug too deep for love
> and I came up with a wife
> whose ways to me are the ways
> of a snake to a man.
>
> It wounds my heart much
> when I imagine what that man Makoka
> does to my wife.
> It torments me to imagine Makoka
> riding my wife, working on her keenly,
> sweating over my wife, both of them
> skin to skin,
> flesh to flesh, both naked
> like fish
> and my wife's legs apart
> generously!
>
> That kind of thing boils my head
> day after day,
> night after night, and
> in the end I cease to be a human being
> but an animal.
> These doings between Makoka and my wife
> have tempted me often
> to murder Makoka.

This Makoka sleeps with my wife
because she's beautiful, and
because he has lots of money to himself
while I have poverty to myself.[3]

The self-pitying plaint of the Kommon Man is not unlike the lament of p'Bitek's Lawino, but the quality of the commentary as well as of the verse has obviously declined.

This decline is even more conspicuous in the works of Maillu's followers, several of whom have been published by Comb books, the company Maillu founded on the profits of his first self-published books. Maina Allan's *One by One* (1975), written "with a touch by David G. Maillu," purports to be the revelations of a village nymphomaniac, and Jasinta Mote's *The Flesh: Part One* (1975), advertised as translated and "produced by David G. Maillu," supposedly contains the true confessions of a prostitute. Muthoni Likimani's *What Does a Man Want?* (1974), a product of the East African Literature Bureau, is a less salacious account of the battle of the sexes, but Muli Mutiso's *Sugar Babies* (1975), which was brought out by Transafrica Publishers after being turned down by Comb Books as "too sexy,"[4] records in robust detail the story of a depraved middle-aged civil servant who tries to copulate with every female who crosses his uninhibited path. The publisher's blurb calls this book "an explosive tour-de-force [which is] frank and humorous [but] on another level...is a tragic commentary on the sexual anarchy and sordid degradation of a society increasingly dominated by lust." The "tragic" note on which the book ends is the hero's horrified discovery that the good-time girl whose professional services he has enjoyed is his own daughter!

All these volumes of venereal verse employ first-person narration and deal in a humorous manner with a wide range of social as well as sexual phenomena. Indeed, it could be said that in form and satirical strategy they are akin to p'Bitek's *Lawino* and other songs, particularly *Song of Malaya*, which is also sung by a prostitute. But they are distant cousins, not direct descendants. David Maillu, the fourth most influential force in East African literature, has intervened and given this poetic medium his own indelible stamp. In the process he has vulgarized p'Bitek's serious humor in order to achieve coarser effects, thereby further popularizing an already popular form by distorting and trivializing it.

Maillu is also the heir apparent of the Charles Mangua tradition. In his prose works he deals with wastrels who ruin their lives by overindulging in sex and alcohol. Usually his heroes are Nairobi civil servants or white-collar workers with a voracious appetite for women, especially office secretaries willing to do literally anything to retain a job or earn a promotion. And usually these jaded bureaucrats suffer for their sins, ultimately losing their overpaid sinecures in the civil service and thereby forfeiting riches, reputation and respectability. They are high class rogues brought low by loose living, picaros of the paperwork empire.

A few examples will illustrate how Maillu exploits this formula. His first "mini-novel," appropriately entitled *Unfit for Human Consumption* (1973), focuses on the misadventures of Jonathan Kinama, a government civil servant whose troubles begin when he is discovered to be sleeping regularly with his roommate's girlfriend. A vicious fight ensues between the two men and Kinama winds up in the hospital for two months. Upon recovering, he withdraws all his money from the bank, gets roaring drunk, and falls prey to a prostitute who robs him of virtually everything. He drinks more in order to ease the pain of this loss, arrives at his office tipsy, and explains to his boss that he has been drinking because he has just been informed of the death of one of his two children back in the village. But then his wife unexpectedly turns up at the office with both children in tow and starts to make a wild scene. When Kinama later learns that he has been fired from his job, he hangs himself.

A more recent example of the same kind of story is Maillu's *No!* (1976), a mini-novel with a senior civil servant as its protagonist. Washington Ndava takes advantage of his position to enrich himself and to seduce the wife of one of his underlings, but the jealous underling hires a gang to exact his revenge. When Ndava and the wife are in bed together, the gang breaks down the locked door of their apartment and assaults him, cutting off his ears and penis. Ndava survives, but after being deserted by his own wife, loses his will to live. He tries to commit suicide by banging his head against a wall, begging his faithful driver to chop off his head with an axe, and crashing his car into a lorry, but nothing seems to work. He only manages to lose an eye and an arm in the process. However, our disintegrating hero eventually succeeds in taking his life by driving his car at high speed into a three-storey building. His faithful driver marries his grief-stricken wife.

Maillu's books are extremely popular among office workers in Nairobi and among young people in rural areas who aspire to live and work in the city. Each new title has sold between 10,000 and 50,000 copies in a year or two, and profits on sales have been so good that within three years Maillu has been able to expand Comb Books from a one-man vanity press to a thriving publishing house employing seven or eight workers who do all the editing, typesetting, layout and design work using the most modern publishing equipment. Maillu estimates that he is probably the most popular of all East African writers, and he has his own sales figures and readership surveys to back up this claim. Since he personally has written at least ten of the sixteen or more titles published by Comb Books, no one else can take credit for the extraordinary commercial success his press achieved in three short years. Comb Books is an indigenous East African publishing phenomenon, and Maillu has been the driving force behind it from the start.

What makes his books so popular? Maillu says he has beeen praised by readers for "hitting the nail on the head"[5] – that is, for depicting life in East Africa as it really is, so people can recognize themselves and their world in his works. He also attempts to write simply, frankly and humorously so as to appeal to the widest possible audience. Moreover, his books are topical and moralistic; they teach as well as entertain. And he is not afraid of dealing as explicitly with sex as with any other vital human experience.

The simplicity, vigor and humor of Maillu's writing can be seen quite clearly in his descriptions of characters in a state of great emotional excitement. Here is Kinama in *Unfit for Human Consumption*, suddenly afraid that the lie he has just told his boss is about to be discovered:

> Kinama opened his mouth and took a heavy breath. A knife went cutting through his spine. His hair moved. His testicles went up and his penis shrunk with the fear of what might happen. His shoes went wet with sweat. His eyebrows began pulling apart and the beer in his stomach began evaporating.[6]

These are vivid and entertaining descriptive details but Maillu's early books were probably more notorious for their zesty love scenes which were presented with the same enthusiastic attention to extraordinary anatomical particularities.

> "Is the door locked up?" she asked him.
> "Yes," he said receiving her with fever, pulling her to himself. His serious thing wetting her thighs generously, he cupped her breasts and massaged them. A heavy breathing took life in the bed. He grabbed a pillow and placed it under her hips, raising them to a perfect vantage, her hands hanging around his neck. He lowered himself and his penis went out the wrong way. She ran her hand and reached it, a warm pestle with much life in it, then directed it into her twitching wet flesh. He felt it touch the warmth and ran smoothly as Anita gave way in, swallowing it until she reached the utmost length. It filled up, burning her and producing electrical effect which sent out such electronic signals out of which life is born. She took her legs up, almost touching his head and gained inside her any millimetre of his that could still be out. Then he pushed his hands under her arms till they met below her neck. He began his wild thrusts, each outward and inward thrust highly punctuated by her groans. She joined him with unique stirring thrusts accompanied by the quivering movements you might have seen from Baganda women dancers. Muscles cracked as his huge thing went on combing and turning her clitoris in every direction. There was a knocking echoing at the back of her brain. She began crying, stirring her thing,

lowering and lifting her pelvis, then taking it higher and higher. He withheld the thrusts to delay the climax. The groaning faded out.[7]

Perhaps one can now understand why Maillu's books attract readers. One can also guess why they eventually were banned by the Tanzanian government.

There is only one short step separating Maillu's muscular melodramas from the dismal depths of unadulterated pornography, and it was perhaps inevitable that someone in East Africa should carry literary lovemaking to its logical commercial extreme. This someone was Bingu Matata (probably a pseudonym) whose disorganized novels of whoredom, *Love for Sale* and *Free Love*, were published in 1975 by a new Nairobi publisher called Vitabu Guliad, possibly an Asian firm. *Love for Sale*, "dedicated to the 'end-of-the-month-fuckers',"[8] did so well in its first year that it was quickly reprinted with a new cover and a 25% higher tag price. *Free Love*, "dedicated to the 'end-of-the-month-drinkers',"[9] carried an announcement that Bingu Matata's third book *Hot Love* would soon be available. There seems to be a ready market for red-light fiction in Nairobi, and Bingu Matata and Vitabu Guliad may be only a portent of the commercial sexploitation to come.

Not all the latest developments in East African publishing are in the direction of tasteless pornography, however. Reputable publishers are beginning to flirt with the street literature reading public by bringing out inexpensive paperbacks featuring stories of love, adventure and mystery. In 1974 Transafrica Publishers started a monthly pamphlet series called Afromance which dealt with the romantic entanglements of young urban African women. Novelettes such as *Hesitant Love, Love Music, Love and Learn, First Love* and *Prescription: Love* told stories of airline stewardesses, singers, university students and nurses who suffer a few momentary setbacks but finally win the man they ardently love. In 1975 the East African branch of Heinemann Educational Books launched their Spear Books series with four titles which are more or less self-explanatory: *Sugar Daddy's Lover, Mystery Smugglers, Lover in the Sky*, and *A Girl Cannot Go On Laughing All the Time*. Intent on capturing a part of the popular literature market, Heinemann a year later released their second handful of Spears: *The Ivory Merchant* (about ivory smuggling), *A Brief Assignment* (about the misadventures of a gang of Nairobi burglars), *A Taste of Business* (about a love affair between an inept businessman and an efficient airline stewardess), and *The Love Root* (about an impotent doctor who gets into amusing difficulties when trying to cure himself with bush medicine). Several of these hundred-page paperbacks have been written by well-known East African authors such as Samuel Kahiga and Mwangi Ruheni, a factor which may help to boost their sales. Heinemann have also been trying their best to make the books more attractive to readers; the major visible difference between the first set of Spear Books and the second is that the covers were changed from colorful cartoons to cheesecake photography, a change brought about by readers' complaints that the first set looked too childish and unsophisticated. Nairobi readers apparently wanted something more urbane for their money, perhaps something more like what was being offered by the Kenya branch of Longman. In 1975 Longman Kenya issued two popular paperbacks: Hilary Ng'weno's *The Men from Pretoria*, a James Bond-type thriller involving a Nairobi crime reporter who uncovers an exciting but dangerous story of international intrigue, and Muli wa Kyendo's *Whispers*, a tear-jerker about a Nairobi secretary who gets trapped in an unhappy marriage. In the same year Longman Uganda brought out as one of the first titles in a new African Creative Writing Series Omunjakko Nakibimbiri's *The Sobbing Sounds*, a picaresque tale of a randy young man's initiation into manhood. The Mangua tradition is obviously still alive and well somewhere in this mass of indigenous pulp.

It is perhaps too early to estimate the commercial success of these numerous experiments in local popular publishing, but the impact that such books are going to have on the direction of the literary movement in East Africa seems clear enough already. The literary desert, after a slow and tentative initial flowering, is now germinating its first full harvest of weeds. Some of these new hothouse mutants will survive and undoubtedly thrive in the Nairobi literary climate; others will die out and disappear. The important questions for the future may well be: can East Africa sustain a wholesome variety of literary efflorescence or will it be increasingly dominated by the coarser vegetables and saplings? Will the proliferation of popular literature crowd out or stunt the serious writings? Will new writers be inclined to produce pap for easy publication and easy money or will they strive to communicate socially relevant messages in complex literary forms? The answers to these questions will ultimately determine whether the desert will be transformed into a healthy garden or a sick wasteland.

NOTES

1. Taban lo Liyong, *The Last Word: Cultural Synthesism* (Nairobi: East African Publishing House, 1969), pp. 25-26.

2. Okot p'Bitek, *Song of Lawino* (Nairobi: East African Publishing House, 1966), pp. 22-24.

3. David G. Maillu, *The Kommon Man: Part One* (Nairobi: Comb Books, 1975), pp. 7-8.

4. Bernth Lindfors, "Interview with John Nottingham," *African Book Publishing Record,* 5 (1979), 84.

5. Bernth Lindfors, "Interview with David Maillu,"*African Book Publishing Record,* 5 (1979), 87.

6. *Unfit for Human Consumption* (Nairobi: Comb Books, 1973), p. 61.

7. Title page of Bingu Matata, *Love for Sale* (Nairobi: Vitabu Guliad, 1975).

8. Title page of Bingu Matata, *Free Love* (Nairobi: Vitabu Guliad, 1975).

Field research for this study was carried out in East Africa in July and August of 1976 on a National Endowment for the Humanities Summer Stipend. I wish to thank both NEH and the English Department of the University of Texas at Austin for their support of this project.

WORKS CITED

Allan, Maina. *One by One*. Nairobi: Comb Books, 1975.

Alot, Magaga. *A Girl Cannot Go On Laughing All the Time*. Nairobi: Spear Books, 1975.

Asalache, Khadambi. *A Calabash of Life*. London: Longman, 1967.

Bobito, Jennifer. *Prescription: Love*. Nairobi: East African Publishing House, 1969.

Buruga, Joseph. *The Abandoned Hut*. Nairobi: East African Publishing House, 1969.

Gicheru, Mwangi. *The Ivory Merchant*. Nairobi: Spear Books, 1976.

Kahiga, Samuel. *Lover in the Sky*. Nairobi: Spear Books, 1975.

Kalitera, Aubrey. *A Taste of Business*. Nairobi: Spear Books, 1976.

Karoki, John. *The Land is Ours*. Nairobi: East African Literature Bureau, 1970.

Kibera, Leonard and Samuel Kahiga. *Potent Ash*. Nairobi: East African Publishing House, ca. 1967.

Kise, Mary. *Love and Learn*. Nairobi: Transafrica Publishers, 1974.

——. *First Love*. Transafrica Publishers, 1974.

Kyendo, Muli wa. *Whispers*. Nairobi: Longman, 1975.

Likimani, Muthoni. *What Does a Man Want?* Nairobi: East African Literature Bureau, 1974.

Maillu, David G. *Unfit for Human Consumption*. Nairobi: Comb Books, 1973.

——. *My Dear Bottle*. Nairobi: Comb Books, 1973.

——. *After 4:30*. Nairobi: Comb Books, 1973.

——. *The Kommon Man: Part One*. Nairobi: Comb Books, 1975.

——. *The Kommon Man: Part Two*. Nairobi: Comb Books, 1975.

——. *The Kommon Man: Part Three*. Nairobi: Comb Books, 1976.

——. *No!* Nairobi: Comb Books, 1976.

Mangua, Charles. *Son of Woman*. Nairobi: East African Publishing House, 1971.

. *A Tail in the Mouth*. Nairobi: East African Publishing House, 1972.

Matata, Bingu. *Love for Sale*. Nairobi: Vitabu Guliad, 1975.

. *Free Love*. Nairobi: Vitabu Guliad, 1975.

Mote, Jasinta. *The Flesh: Part One*. Nairobi: Comb Books, 1975.

Mutiso, Muli. *Sugar Babies*. Nairobi: Transafrica Publishers, 1975.

Mwangi, Meja. *Carcase for Hounds*. London: Heinemann, 1974.

. *Taste of Death*. Nairobi: East African Publishing House, 1975.

Nakibimbiri, Omunjakko. *The Sobbing Sounds*. n.p.: Longman Uganda, 1975.

Ndii, Ayub. *A Brief Assignment*. Nairobi: Spear Books, 1976.

Ngubiah, S. N. *A Curse from God*. Nairobi: East African Literature Bureau, 1970.

Ngugi wa Thiong'o (James Ngugi). *Weep Not, Child*. London: Heinemann, 1964.

. *The River Between*. London: Heinemann, 1965.

. *A Grain of Wheat*. London: Heinemann, 1967.

Ng'weno, Hilary. *The Men from Pretoria*. Nairobi: Longman Kenya, 1975.

Oculi, Okello. *Orphan*. Nairobi: East African Publishing House, 1968.

. *Prostitute*. Nairobi: East African Publishing House, 1968.

Ogot, Grace. *The Promised Land*. Nairobi: East African Publishing House, 1966.

Owino, Rosemarie. *Sugar Daddy's Lover*. Nairobi: Spear Books, 1975.

p'Bitek, Okot. *Song of Lawino*. Nairobi: East African Publishing House, 1970.

. *Song of Ocol*. Nairobi: East African Publishing House, 1970.

. *Two Songs*. Nairobi: East African Publishing House, 1971.

Ruheni, Mwangi. *Mystery Smugglers*. Nairobi: Spear Books, 1975.

. *The Love Root*. Nairobi: Spear Books, 1976.

Sousi, Damaris. *Hesitant Love*. Nairobi: Spear Books, 1976.

. *Love Music*. Nairobi: Transafrica Publishers, 1974.

Wachira, Godwin. *Ordeal in the Forest*. Nairobi: East African Publishing House, 1968.

Waciuma, Charity. *Daughter of Mumbi*. Nairobi: East African Publishing House, 1969.

Watene, Kenneth. *My Son for My Freedom and Other Plays*. Nairobi: East African Publishing House, 1973.

. *Dedan Kimathi*. Nairobi: Transafrica Publishers, 1974.

The Songs of Okot p'Bitek

When Okot p'Bitek surprised the world with *Song of Lawino* in 1966, he was recognized immediately as a major African poet. No other African writer – except possibly Christopher Okigbo of Nigeria – had made such an indelible impact with his first volume of verse, creating at one stroke a new poetic idiom so entirely his own. Most African poets writing in English and French were cultural mulattoes seeking self-consciously to fuse the two disparate traditions of verbal creativity on which they had been nurtured. Senghor, for instance, certainly owed as much to French surrealism as he did to the songs of the Serer; Okigbo was directly descended from Pound, Eliot and Peter Thomas as well as from anonymous Igbo bards; and J. P. Clark had deliberately imitated the techniques of Hopkins, Dylan Thomas, Japanese haiku and Ijaw oral art while forging his early apprentice verse. But Okot p'Bitek was refreshingly different. When he sang, no European echoes could be heard in the background. His *Song of Lawino* was the first long poem in English to achieve a totally different African identity.

This was no accident, considering Okot's education, cultural interests and literary inclinations. After attending high school in Uganda, earning a Certificate of Education at Bristol University and studying law at the University of Wales in Aberystwyth, he went on to Oxford where he worked for a B. Litt. at the Institute of Social Anthropology. It was here that he wrote a thesis on Acoli and Lango traditional songs, a formal academic study which must have forced him to take a closer look at the structure, content and style of songs he had heard and sung as a young man growing up in Uganda.[1] This project, completed three years before the publication of *Song of Lawino*, may have suggested to him a new way of singing in English.

Okot appears to have developed an interest in music, song, literature and traditional culture while very young and to have sustained this interest throughout his life. As a schoolboy at King's College Budo he composed and produced an opera, and in 1953, when only twenty-two years old, he published his first literary work, *Lak tar miyo kinyero wi lobo* (Are your teeth white? Then laugh), a novel in Acoli. After completing his undergraduate education in Britain, he returned to Uganda and joined the staff of the Extra-Mural Department at Makerere University College, a job which enabled him to carry out further research on the oral literature of the peoples of northern Uganda and to found and organize an annual Gulu Festival of the Arts. In 1966 he was appointed Director of the Uganda National Theatre and Cultural Centre in Kampala, where he did much to promote local cultural activities. At the end of 1967 he joined the Western Kenya section of Nairobi University College's Extra-Mural Department and immediately became the moving force behind the first Kisumu Arts Festival held in December, 1968. Then, in the academic year 1969-70, he accepted a one-year appointment as Fellow in the International Writing Program at the University of Iowa, a position which enabled him to write full time. A year later he became attached to the University of Nairobi as Research Fellow at the Institute of African Studies and part-time Lecturer in Sociology and Literature. He remained at the University of Nairobi until 1978, a year during which he held visiting appointments at both the University of Texas at Austin and the University of Ife in Nigeria. In 1979, after Idi Amin Dada was overthrown, he returned once more to Makerere University, where initially he was associated with the Institute of Social Research.[2] In February 1982 he was appointed the first Professor of Creative Writing in the Department of Literature, and he died at his home in Kampala only five months later at the age of 51.

Throughout his busy academic and professional career, Okot p'Bitek never stopped writing. His enormously successful *Song of Lawino* was soon followed by three other long poems of the same genre: *Song of Ocol* (1970), "Song of Prisoner" and "Song of Malaya" (the latter two were published together in *Two Songs*, 1971).[3] He also published two scholarly works, *African Religions in Western Scholarship* (1971) and *Religion of the Central Luo* (1971), one of which may have been written originally as his D. Phil. thesis in religion at Oxford.[4] His interest in oral forms of literature was reflected in publication of *Horn of My Love* (1974), a collection of Acoli songs; *Hare and Hornbill* (1978), a collection of folktales; and *Acoli Proverbs* (1985).

Another book, *Africa's Cultural Revolution* (1973) which was a collection of some of the essays he wrote for East African periodicals, magazines and newspapers between 1964 and 1971, contains several of Okot's most candid statements on African culture, so it serves as an excellent introduction to some of the ideas embedded in his poetry. In the preface to *Africa's Cultural Revolution* Okot says that his essays are part of the revolutionary struggle in Africa "dedicated to the total demolition of foreign cultural domination and the restoration and promotion of Africa's proud culture to its rightful place." In order to achieve these worthwhile nationalistic goals,

Africa must re-examine herself critically. She must discover her true self, and rid herself of all "apemanship". For only then can she begin to develop a culture of her own. Africa must redefine all cultural terms according to her own interests. As she has broken the political bondage of colonialism, she must continue the economic and cultural revolution until she refuses to be led by the nose by foreigners. We must also reject the erroneous attempts of foreign students to interpret and present her. We must interpret and present Africa in our own way, in our own interests.[5]

Okot's aim as a writer is to assist in this vital task of cultural redefinition.

Okot's essays range widely over such varied topics as literature, philosophy, religion, politics, history, education, sex and pop music. But underlying them all is an insistence on the validity and dignity of indigenous African culture. Okot wants Africans – especially educated Africans – to accept their Africanness and stop mimicking non-African customs, traditions, fashions and styles which are entirely inappropriate and even a bit ridiculous in an African setting. Only by affirming the integrity of their own cultural identity will Africans find happiness and genuine fulfillment. As Ngugi wa Thiong'o puts it in an introduction to these essays, Okot "is simply and rightly saying that we cannot ape and hope to create."[6] Okot desires to release the creative potential of Africa by making Africans conscious and proud of their own rich cultural heritage.

In his essays on literature, Okot begins the process of cultural redefinition by questioning the Western conception of literature itself. He points out that "in Western scholarship, literature means the writings of a particular time or country, especially those valued for excellence of form or expression. This definition, with its emphasis on 'writing', implies that literature is the exclusive preserve of human societies which have invented the art of writing."[7] In place of this "narrow and discriminatory definition" Okot advocates adopting a more "dynamic and democratic" notion of literature as an art embracing "all the creative works of man expressed in words."[8] This would take in oral as well as written performances because "words can be spoken, sung or written. The voice of the singer or the speaker and the pen and paper are mere midwives of a pregnant mind. A song is a song whether it is sung, spoken or written down."[9] By redefining literature in this way, Okot is able to demonstrate that Africa possesses one of the richest literary cultures in the world.

He also emphasizes that literature in Africa is a living social art. It is not a collection of old classics that one reads alone or studies diligently at school in order to pass examinations and win certificates. It is an intensely expressive activity which aims at publicly communicating deeply felt emotions. Sometimes it may be designed to amuse, sometimes to instruct, but the best literature never fails to make a profound impact on the whole community. It is a totally democratic art which attempts to reach everyone within earshot. There must always be direct communication between the artist and his audience and full participation by all present. This means that the African literary artist cannot afford to indulge in deliberate obscurity. He produces his art not for art's sake but for society's sake.

Song of Lawino was created in this spirit. It is a thoroughly indigenous poem in form, content, style, message and aesthetic philosophy. Okot took the songs he knew best – Acoli and Lango traditional songs of praise and abuse, joy and sorrow, sympathy and satire – and made use of their rich poetic resources in composing an original anthem in honor of Africa. The result was something both old and new because while Okot exploited many of the conventions of oral art, he also invented a novel literary genre which had never been seen in African writing before. He did this first in his own mother tongue and then in English, claiming to have "clipped a bit of the eagle's wings and rendered the sharp edges of the warrior's sword rusty and blunt, and also murdered rhythm and rhyme"[10] in the process of translation. Like a traditional poet he was trying to reach the widest possible audience because he felt he had an important idea to impart. And like a literary artist he was still experimenting with his verbal medium in an effort to find a uniquely appropriate idiom to carry his message. *Song of Lawino* is thus a hybrid achievement, a successful sustained blending of oral and literary art in a long poem remarkably innovative in conception and design yet immanently Afican in orientation.

Much of the Africanness of the poem resides in its imagery, ideology and rhetorical structure. It is an oral song sung by an illiterate Ugandan housewife who complains bitterly about the insults and ill treatment she receives from her university-trained husband. Being an unschooled village girl, Lawino speaks in the earthy idiom of the rural peasantry and sees everything from the perspective of a country cousin. She cannot understand why her husband Ocol follows Western ways and why he rejects her for clinging to the traditions of her people. She knows nothing about ballroom dancing, cooking on a modern stove, and reading clocks, books or thermometers, and sees no reason why she should learn such strange skills when she can get along perfectly well without them. She has been exposed to a few Christian beliefs and teachings but these she found either incomprehensible or profoundly perplexing. Why can't she be allowed to follow her own ways? Why must Ocol abuse and punish her for being African? These are the questions Lawino asks repeatedly as she recounts her husband's brutality and cruel words. Recalling the time Ocol branded her and her kinsfolk as ignorant, superstitious fools, she laments:

My husband's tongue
Is bitter like the roots of the *lyonno* lily,
It is hot like the penis of the bee,
Like the sting of the *kalang*!
Ocol's tongue is fierce like the arrow of the scorpion,
Deadly like the spear of the buffalo-hornet.
It is ferocious
Like the poison of a barren woman
And corrosive like the juice of the gourd. (p. 16)

Everything Lawino says is rooted in the reality she has mastered, the world she knows. She speaks in a language which reveals an intimate knowledge and experience of rural African life. Obviously such a perceptive observer is neither ignorant nor foolishly superstitious. Lawino's imagery alone refutes Ocol's accusation.

Okot's strategy throughout the poem is to contrast the natural grace and dignity of traditional African ways with the groteque artificiality of modern habits and practices that educated Africans have copied from Europe. The primary target is Ocol's "apemanship" but Okot gradually widens the focus of Lawino's complaints to embrace much larger social, political and religious issues arising from rabid, unthinking Westernization. Okot once described *Song of Lawino* in an interview as

a big laugh by this village girl called Lawino, laughing at modern man and modern woman in Uganda. She thinks that the educated folk are spoiled, in the sense that they don't belong, they don't enjoy fully the culture of the people of Uganda, and she thinks that if only these educated people could stop a little bit and look back into the village they would find a much richer life altogether.[11]

Lawino is able to provide a window on both African worlds because she is the product of one and a prisoner in the other. Like Alice in Wonderland, like Gulliver, like Medza in Beti's *Mission to Kala*, she discovers herself in a strange new universe and reacts strongly to anything that deviates from her own cultural expectations and prejudices. But a major difference in her case is that most of her audience – Western as well as African – does not share her cultural perspective but rather that of Ocol, the modern man she is laughing at. She forces such readers to see themselves from an entirely different point of view and to join in the laughter. By mirroring modern manners through her own distorted ethnocentric lens, Lawino serves as a catalyst of satire.

But she also becomes a victim of satire because occasionally there are significant discrepancies between her words and deeds. For instance, after beginning a devastating assault on the appearance of Ocol's modern girlfriend Clementine, she pauses briefly to assure her audience that her motives are pure:

> Do not think I am insulting
> The woman with whom I share my husband!
> Do not think my tongue
> Is being sharpened by jealousy
> It is the sight of Tina
> That provokes sympathy from my heart.
>
> I do not deny
> I am a little jealous.
> It is no good lying,
> We all suffer from a little jealousy.
> It catches you unawares
> Like the ghosts that bring fevers;
> It surprises people
> Like earth tremors:
> But when you see the beautiful woman
> With whom I share my husband
> You feel a little pity for her! (pp. 24-25)

She then resumes her attack with gusto, ridiculing Tina's dried-up breasts and padded brassiere, insinuating she has aborted or killed many children in her long lifetime, and scoffing at her slim "meatless" figure. Obviously, Lawino is more than a little jealous of the woman she claims to pity.

Okot carefully counterpoints Lawino's lapses into pure invective with her gentle, nostalgic reflections on traditional African life. These frequent changes in mood and tempo reveal the softer side of her personality while reinforcing her emphasis on differences between the old and the new. Lawino's sympathies always lie with tradition, and through graphic images and telling details she is able to communicate her enthusiasm for the customs and practices of her people. She describes a civilization which is wholesome, coherent, deeply satisfying to those born in it, and therefore naturally resistant to fundamental change. Her angry tirade against Tina is followed by a rosy account of how rivals for a man's love behave in Acoli society and then by a level-headed appeal to Ocol politely asking him to come to his senses and stop rejecting his own heritage.

> Listen Ocol, my friend,
> The ways of your ancestors
> Are good,
> Their customs are solid
> And not hollow

They are not thin, not easily breakable
They cannot be blown away
By the winds
Because their roots reach deep into the soil. (p. 29)

This is the theme of Lawino's entire song.

But because she tends to sing it too stridently, because she refuses to make the slightest effort to adjust to modern ways, because she remains so intractably old-fashioned, Lawino eventually exposes herself as a tribal chauvinist who is as limited in vision as her husband Ocol. Sometimes she is conscious of her inflexibility, as when she admits she cannot "cook like a white woman" or "dance the white man's dances" because she has never cared to learn such revolting skills. On other occasions she appears to be totally unaware of the strength of her own cultural prejudices, and this naiveté sets her criticism of others in an ironic light. For example she showers insults on Tina's lipstick, powder, perfume, wig, and artificially dyed and straightened hair yet in the very next breath goes on to extol Acoli customs of tattooing, body-painting, body-scenting and hair dressing. Her aim may be to condemn Tina's apewomanship and to ridicule Ocol's perverse preference for Western odors and adornments, but she does not seem to realize that she is simultaneously betraying the absurdity of her own dogmatic Acolitude. Her unconscious underscoring of her own argument is a classic example of reflexive satire: the use of satire to satirize the satirist.

This is not to say that her attacks on the follies of Westernized Africans are invalid or unjustified. Lawino has a keen eye for human stupidity, and her common sense does not allow her to be easily taken in by pretense and affectation. She views Ocol and Tina not as her superiors but as ordinary human beings who are struggling desperately to prove themselves superior by adopting Western ways. Since she does not understand such ways, she raises fundamental questions about their logic and propriety which Westerners and Westernized Africans never bother to ask. For instance, she wants to know why

At the height of the hot season
The progressive and civilized ones
Put on blanket suits
And woolen socks from Europe,
Long under-pants
And woolen vests,
White shirts;
They wear dark glasses
And neck-ties from Europe. (p. 37)

She also cannot imagine what pleasure these people take in smoking, drinking, kissing, and other unclean, unnatural acts. Lawino regards such habits as foolish and unhealthy. Those who indulge in them ought to be avoided, not admired or emulated.

Even more difficult for Lawino to fathom are Western habits of mind. Why should Ocol reckon time by consulting a clock when there are much more natural signs by which to measure the passing of a day? Why should he want to give his children Christian names when Acoli names are more meaningful? Why should he place so much faith in Western medicine and prayer and scorn the remedies offered by herbalists and diviners? Why should politicians who are working toward the same goals oppose one another? By asking these questions Lawino focuses attention on some of the arbitrary and seemingly irrational aspects of Western behavior which would very likely baffle any non-Westerner encountering them for the first time. She forces us to recognize the illogicality of our ways. Her incomprehension is both a warning and a protest against cultural arrogance.

What makes Lawino a more sensible person than Ocol is her acceptance of the validity of other cultures, despite her personal aversion to them. She does not insist, as Ocol does, that everyone conform to her own cultural pattern. She realizes that Westerners will behave as Westerners, and though she would clearly prefer Africans to behave as Africans, she is content to let Ocol eat Western food and adopt Western eccentricities so long as he reciprocates with equal tolerance for her traditional preferences. She would like to see her husband return to the Acoli life style he had once enjoyed, but if that is impossible (as it appears to be), then let him at least respect her right to remain loyal to the ways of her ancestors. At one point she sums it all up by saying

> I do not understand
> The ways of foreigners
> But I do not despise their customs.
> Why should you despise yours?...
> The pumpkin in the old homestead
> Must not be uprooted! (pp. 29-30)

Lawino's lament is a plea for tolerance, understanding and respect for African culture.

The success of *Song of Lawino* rests primarily on Okot's creation of a convincing persona to articulate his ideas. Lawino's vibrant personality animates the entire poem, giving it the energy and earthiness appropriate to an iconoclastic assault on postcolonial "high" culture. Only a woman of her peasant origins could reject Westernization so totally. Only a scorned wife of her particular matrimonial temper could denounce her husband so passionately yet yearn to win back his love. There may be inconsistencies in her conduct and huge self-contradictions in her argument, but these simply make her a more believable human being. She wins us over by the honest eloquence of her emotion, the primitive force of her tongue.

Yet we must never forget that she is a person and that Okot may not share all her views. *Song of Lawino* is a long dramatic monologue deliberately placed in the mouth of an invented character, and to understnd its full meaning, we must carefully appraise the singer as well as the song. Lawino presents a persuasive case for African tradition because she is able to perceive salient absurdities of modern African life through eyes unclouded by formal education or acculturation to Western ways. But though she sees clearly, her vision is limited by her own narrow cultural prejudices to a single, circumscribed point of view, and she has real difficulty seeing beyond her Acoli nose. This makes a good deal of her testimony suspect, for it is impossible to trust impassioned polemics brimming with so much overstatement and exaggeration. Lawino's argument, though tempered with unconscious irony, is just too one-sided.

This may have been why Okot decided to write *Song of Ocol* as a reply to Lawino. By giving Ocol a chance to state his own case, Okot could examine the same social, political and cultural issues from a totally different point of view. And in the process of ostensibly redressing the balance of a biased conjugal debate, he could make clever use of satire to reassert basically the same position he had advocated in *Song of Lawino*.

In singing his song, Ocol reveals himself as exactly the type of person Lawino had described – an angry, insensitive, impatient opportunist intent on destroying African traditions and institutions in the name of progress. He hates everything black because he associates blackness with backwardness and primitivism.

> What is Africa?
> To me?
>
> Blackness,
> Deep, deep fathomless
> Darkness;
>
> Africa,
> Idle giant
> Basking in the sun,
> Sleeping, snoring,
> Twitching in dreams;
>
> Diseased with a chronic illness,
> Choking with black ignorance,

Chained to the rock
Of poverty...

Mother, mother,
Why,
Why was I born
Black? (pp. 19-22)

In order to overcome his feelings of self-hatred and inferiority, Ocol is ready to uproot Lawino's pumpkins, burn mud huts, imprison witches and village poets, hang professors of African studies and obliterate indigenous cultural treasures. His aim is to

Smash all these mirrors
That I may not see
The blackness of the past
From which I came
Reflected in them. (p. 31)

Much of Ocol's song is an inventory of what he intends to destroy. He speaks as a member of the ruling class that came to power after independence with the ambition of transforming a former colony into a modern nation state. In order to bring "civilization" to their part of the world, these Westernized African leaders are planning to demolish the Old Homestead and build a New City complete with statues of European explorers, missionaries and kings. Their notion of national progress is further imitation of Europe.

Nothing Ocol says wins our sympathy. He seems so intent on ravaging the countryside and throwing harmless people into prison in order to achieve a worthless goal that it is impossible to view him in a friendly light. He is obviously a blackguard obsessed with a desire to prove himself white. He displays no love or tenderness toward his fellow man and possesses no traits worthy of admiration. Indeed, one wonders why Lawino wants him back!

As Ocol speaks, his own words condemn him, making him the butt of ridicule. For example, after outlining a strategy for wiping out African culture and traditions and replacing them with Western ways, he asks an African Ambassador at the United Nations to

Tell the world
In English or in French,
Talk about
The African foundation
On which we are

Building the new nations
Of Africa. (p. 83)

Ocol also claims to hate poverty but does nothing to help the poor, even though he has grown wealthy as a politician. His major concern as a public servant is not with the public welfare but with keeping thieves and trespassers off his vast country estate. He is a rich landed aristocrat in a poor underdeveloped country, a contrast which points up the disparity between his nationalistic ideals and parasitic practices. Virtually every line he speaks betrays him as an arch-hypocrite.

By the time we finish *Song of Ocol* we are aware that Lawino was right: Ocol's "apemanship" has turned him into a monster. If he had managed to retain a healthy respect for African traditions, he might have been a better person and a far more constructive influence on his society. His fanatical Westernization and rejection of himself have prevented him from developing into a creative human being. He has lost not just his ethnic identity but his humanity.

Thus *Song of Lawino* and *Song of Ocol*, though structured as a debate, actually present two sides of the same coin: they may face in opposite directions but they have precisely the same ring. Ocol's argument is undercut so completely by irony that it reinforces Lawino's position.. And Okot, by removing himself from the quarrel between his personae, is able to establish an independent stance some distance from the ground Lawino defends. He advocates neither an atavistic return to Acoli customs and traditions nor a total abandonment of Western ways. His aim appears to be to help educated Africans – his readers, in fact – appreciate their rich cultural heritage so they can create a new culture equally meaningful and relevant to Africa.

Okot's next song was much more ambiguous. Instead of carrying the cultural debate further, he turned to an explosive new political subject and treated it in a deliberately equivocal fashion. He used the same basic poetic form – an emotionally charged dramatic monologue – but invested it with such complex irony that its moral center was difficult to discern. The poem has aroused considerable controversy in East Africa[12] and is likely to go on provoking lively discussion for some time to come. Brief and puzzling, it has all the fascination of a conundrum.

"Song of Prisoner" begins as the anguished soliloquy of a man who appears to have been brutally beaten and thrown into prison for the most trivial of offenses: vagrancy and loitering in the City Park. As he sits there counting his wounds and cursing his captors, he seems a victim of injustice and oppression. He broods on thoughts of his starving children, complains of his own hunger and thirst, and frequently lashes out at those he imagines to be responsible for his misfortunes. He even goes so far as to accuse his dead father of not having married a woman from the right clan, thereby foisting bad genes on all his descendants; then he turns around and accuses his mother of the same catastrophic matrimonial misjudgement. He also imagines his wife to be sleeping with a "Big Chief" who drives a Mercedes Benz, and this vision gives him a macabre urge to "drink human blood" and "eat human liver" (pp. 46-47). Imprisonment obviously is driving him insane.

Not until the middle of the poem do we learn the real reason he has been locked up: he is a hired assassin who has killed the Head of State. Though he claims to have done this out of love for his country, his charge that the leader was a "traitor, a dictator, a murderer, a racist, a tribalist, a clannist, a brotherist...a reactionary, a revisionist, a fat black capitalist, an extortioner, an exploiter" (pp. 67-68) sounds suspiciously like programmatic revolutionary rhetoric. Perhaps the prisoner is the heroic liberator he claims to be; perhaps he is the dupe of sinister forces in his society. In evaluating his conduct, we have only his own half-demented words to go by.

And next we hear him shouting that he had been a Minister in the Government, in fact had been the one responsible for "Law and Order...Peace and Goodwill in the Land" (p. 83). He asks for his gold pen so he can write his children and parents and send them fat cheques. He now appears to have changed character completely, picking up a new set of parents along the way and leapfrogging from the depths of proletarian squalor to the heights of bourgeois luxury. Indeed, he has been transmuted into another Ocol. Could this be the same prisoner we had seen and heard earlier? If so, has he gone irretrievably mad? What accounts for his sudden, magical transformation?

Okot does not stop to answer these questions before moving into the final section of the poem, which contains a morbid appeal for oblivion as a distraction from despair. The prisoner says he wants to be free so he can sing, drink, dance and fornicate until he forgets the anguish of his insignificance. He knows that he has no future and that his children will never go to school or have a chance to escape wretched poverty. His only hope for release from these depressing thoughts lies in total debauchery:

> I want to drink
> And get drunk,
> I do not want to know
> That I am powerless
> and helpless,
> I do not want to remember anything.

I want to forget
That I am a lightless star,
A proud Eagle
Shot down
By the arrow
Of Uhuru! (p. 94)

The poem's internal contradictions generate a confused response. Should we feel sympathy for this prisoner, or disgust? Is he worthy of pity, approbation, or condemnation? Was his crime noble or base? Okot leads us first toward one conclusion, then toward another until we are trapped in the labyrinth of the prisoner's complex personality. By encouraging us to make judgements which we later feel compelled to reverse, Okot makes us realize how difficult it is to distinguish between good and bad in contemporary Africa. We applaud the guerrilla "freedom fighters" who boldly take the law into their own hands, yet we are appalled by the hard-fisted tactics of military regimes founded with the same disregard for individual liberties. The political assassin is seen as a national hero by some and as a self-seeking rogue by others. Many who feel oppressed may themselves be ruthless oppressors. Okot seems to be saying that in the confusion of post-Uhuru Africa, justice, honor, loyalty, morality – all the great social and political virtues – may be subject to reinterpretation according to the exigencies of the moment and the bias of the interpreter. There are no longer any fixed truths, only competing ideologies. This may be a cynical conclusion and perhaps even a gross misreading of Okot's intention, but when confronted with such rich ambiguity in a literary work, it is easy for a reader to go astray. The fact that the poem has already stirred so much controversy suggests that it invites many different interpretations.

Although most critics have assumed that "Song of Prisoner" is the song of a single prisoner,[13] there is some evidence suggesting that it may have been conceived as a medley of various voices. Okot is reported to have said that the "Soft Grass" episode involving the Minister and the gold pen is an interpolation by "a man in the next cell, whom the Prisoner overhears."[14] If this is so, what is to prevent us from identifying other lyrics which seem out of character as songs sung by other prisoners? Perhaps "Song of Prisoner" actually represents the communal wailings of an entire cell block. This would make the poem less complex psychologically but certainly no less damning as an indictment of contemporary African experience. Despite flashes of gallows humor, it remains a very gloomy song.

"Song of Malaya," which is paired with "Song of Prisoner" in *Two Songs*, provides boisterous comic relief. The prostitute who sings it is good natured, proud of her profession and tolerant of all mankind. Like a public comfort station she invites men of every description to enter and make use of her facilities. No one is barred or refused service. She is the great social equalizer, humanity's most effective democratizer because she mixes with high and low indiscriminately. All who come to her are reduced to the same level. She functions as the world's lowest common multiplier.

And for this very reason she is in a good position to expose cant and hypocrisy. Her song is a series of rebukes to her critics – to the chief who accuses her of giving him venereal disease, to the wife who is unhappy about sharing her husband with a whore, to the priest who preaches that monogamy is morality, to the schoolmaster who calls her children bastards, to the brother who despises her yet buys the services of other prostitutes, to the policeman who arrests her even though he was her customer the night before. Malaya answers their charges with common sense and good humor, pointing out their own failings and moral weaknesses in the process. Each of her replies ends with words of encouragement to her fellow professionals and lay workers:

> Sister *Malayas*
> Wherever you are,
> Wealth and health
> To us all. (p. 159)

As in *Song of Lawino* the strategy of the monologue is to juxtapose two different world views, one a commonly accepted perspective and the other a somewhat unorthodox outlook, and to slant the argument in such a fashion as to demonstrate the moral superiority of the latter. In "Song of Malaya" we find ourselves agreeing that prostitution seems a wholesome profession when compared with marriage, priesthood, teaching, law enforcement, and other occupations which are no better ethically and spiritually than the imperfect human beings who take them up. The prostitute is at least self-reliant, open and unpretentious – a much healthier person psychologically than those who condemn her. She embraces all who come to her, never attempting to deny pleasure to those who are willing to pay the price. Her message, like Lawino's, is one of tolerance for human diversity. She accepts whatever seems natural and genuine, rejecting only the patently artificial and perverted. Malaya is clearly more moral than her society.

In *Artist, the Ruler* (1986), a collection of Okot's essays and unfinished works published posthumously, one finds some of the same arguments about culture, art and values that he had espoused earlier. He persisted in raising big questions and seeking to answer them in a way that affirmed the validity of indigenous social and cultural institutions. He also put forward the view that the artist had a key role to play in guiding society toward humane goals. In the essay from which the title of the book was taken, he asserted that

> If there are two types of rulers in every society, that is, those who use physical force to subdue men, and those that employ beautiful things, sweet songs and funny stories, rhythm, shape and colour, to keep individuals and society sane and flourishing, then in my view, it is the artist who is the greater ruler.[15]

The artist thus is not just an entertainer but a gentle leader and legislator of social norms. And who qualifies for this special role in society? In Okot's view, "every human being is an artist."[16] Some may be greater than others, but all respond to beauty, all participate in creating art and investing it with social relevance.

This was not just empty theorizing on Okot's part, for he lived his life according to this credo. As an artist, as an educator, as an agitator, his role was basically the same. He himself was quite conscious of the consistency of his position. In an interview he once said

> I want to suggest that all my writings, whether they are anthropological monographs, studies of religion, essays, songs, poems, or even traditional stories and proverbs such as I am collecting now, all of them are ammunition for one big battle: the battle to decide where we here in Africa are going and what kind of society we are building. I think you will find great similarities in all the different things I have been producing because they all have basically the same aim.[17]

Clearly Okot was quite serious about what he was doing as a writer.

Some of the criticism directed at Okot as a commentator on East African society has asserted that his analysis of contemporary social problems is shallow for he is more an entertainer than an incisive social scientist or political reformer. Taban lo Liyong has charged him with playfulness and insincerity:

> I see more of the frivolous and more of the jester in these [sociological and anthropological] works. Only rarely do I see an Okot with tight lips and protracted visage...Okot with a political temper is better than Okot the sceptic posing as a champion for dying and dead customs he doesn't believe in. These are useful only as means for giving play to sarcasm, and making fun of other people's ways in mock-revenge for their destruction of the ways of his own people, again in which he does not seriously believe.[18]

Ngugi wa Thiong'o has expressed the view that Okot is a bit short-sighted for he fails to look at the root causes of East Africa's social problems:

"While I agree with p'Bitek's call for a cultural revolution, I sometimes feel that he is in danger of emphasizing culture as if it could be divorced from its political and economic basis...Can we be ourselves while our economic life is regulated by forces outside Africa?"[19] Andrew Gurr, echoing Ngugi and quoting Frantz Fanon, has complained that Okot's diagnosis of social ills "does not go below the surface of the problem...[He] is fussing over the outworn garments of the past, not the teeming present."[20] These critics want Okot to probe more deeply into the body politic and expose the sources of its sickness instead of merely mocking the bizarre convulsions of a delirious, moribund society. They would like him to behave as a physician rather than as a clown.

Yet Okot's strident style of satirical singing won him a wider audience than any prescriptive political propaganda would have done, and he has achieved this immense popularity without pulling any of his punches. Indeed, his four outspoken songs compel us to listen to voices we would not ordinarily heed. Original in form, technique and idea, these vivid lyrical soliloquies captivate the imagination and provoke the intellect while advancing half-ironic arguments that radically challenge some of our basic cultural assumptions. Our immediate reaction to such audacity may be to laugh in astonishment, but Okot has a talent for forcing us to think as we laugh. He never lets us rest comfortably in mindless complacency. This makes him an unsettling writer, indeed a very revolutionary artist, for his constant questioning teaches us entirely new ways of seeing ourselves and others. By singing comically and occasionally off-key, he draws attention to serious social disharmonies which require adjustment and correction. He is writing not merely to amuse but to instruct and guide his people. He once said that a truly African literature must have "deep human roots" and deal "honestly and truthfully with the problems of the human situation."[21] Okot p'Bitek, who spent his life striving to produce this kind of literature, deserves recognition as one of Africa's major creative talents. Though he remains to some extent a blithe spirit, he articulated important ideas about culture and identity that still have relevance in Africa today. Okot may have been a clown but he was a serious clown, the kind whose antics provoke wholesome, regenerative laughter.

NOTES

1.   Geroge Heron, in the only full-length study of Okot's work to date, *The Poetry of Okot p'Bitek* (London: Heinemann, 1976), p. 3, notes that "the thesis has very little to say about the literary nature of the songs" but that it served "to renew and consolidate his contact with oral literature, especially through his field work, at a crucial point in his life." Heron carefully examines the nature of Okot's debt to oral literature in this book and in an earlier article, "The Influence of the Rhetoric of Acoli Oral Songs on the Poems of Okot p'Bitek," *Occasional Papers* (Kano) 1, 1 (1975), 22-53. Heron has also prepared a useful study guide, *Notes on Okot p'Bitek's* Song of Lawino *and* Song of Ocol (Nairobi: Heinemann, 1975), and a helpful

"Introduction" to a new combined school edition of *Song of Lawino and Song of Ocol* (Nairobi: East African Publishing House, 1972), pp. 6-35. Okot himself has translated and edited a collection of Acoli oral poetry, *Horn of My Love* (London: Heinemann, 1974), which it is interesting to compare with his own verse.

2.   Biographical information on Okot can be found in Janheinz Jahn, Ulla Schild, and Almut Nordmann, *Who's Who in African Literature: Biographies, Works, Commentaries* (Tübingen: Horst Erdmann, 1972), pp. 313-14; Donald E. Herdeck, *African Authors: A Companion to Black African Writing, Volume I: 1300-1973* (Washington, D.C.: Black Orpheus Press, 1973), pp. 339-40; Cosmo Pieterse and Dennis Duerden, eds., *African Writers Talking* (London: Heinemann, 1972), pp. 149-55; Bernth Lindfors, ed., *Mazungumzo: Interviews with East African Writers, Publishers, Editors and Scholars* (Athens, Ohio: Ohio University Center for International Studies, Africa Program, 1980); and on the book jackets of his poems and scholarly works.

3.   *Song of Lawino* (Nairobi: East African Publishing House, 1966); *Song of Ocol* (Nairobi: East African Publishing House, 1970); *Two Songs* (Nairobi: East African Publishing House, 1971). All quotations are taken from these editions.

4.   *African Religions in Western Scholarship* (Kampala, Nairobi, Dar es Salaam: East African Literature Bureau, n.d.); *Religion of the Central Luo* (Nairobi, Kampala, Dar es Salaam: East African Literature Bureau, 1971). The thesis is mentioned in Pieterse and Duerden, p. 149.

5.   *Africa's Cultural Revolution* (Nairobi: Macmillan Books for Africa, 1973), p. vii.

6.   Ibid., p. xii.

7.   Ibid., p. 18.

8.   Ibid., p. 20.

9.   Ibid.

10.   *Song of Lawino*, p. 6.

11.   Pieterse and Duerden, pp. 149-50.

12.   See, e.g., Atieno-Odhiambo, Aloo Ojuka, Margaret Marshment, and George Heron, "Okot and *Two Songs*, a Discussion," in *Standpoints on African Literature*, ed. Chris L. Wanjala (Nairobi, Kampala, Dar es Salaam: East African Literature Bureau, 1973), pp. 96-146.

13.   The American edition is entitled *Song of a Prisoner* (New York: Third Press, 1971).

14.   *Standpoints on African Literature*, p. 134.

15.   *Artist, the Ruler: Essays on Art, Culture and Values* (Nairobi: Heinemann Kenya, 1986), p. 40.

16.   *Ibid.*, p. 41.

17.   Bernth Lindfors, "An Interviewwith Okot p'Bitek," *World Literature Written in English*, 16 (1977), 291-92.

18.   Taban lo Liyong, *The Last Word: Cultural Synthesism* (Nairobi: East African Publishing House, 1969), pp. 137, 155.

19.   Ngugi wa Thiong'o, "Introduction," *Africa's Cultural Revolution* (Nairobi: Macmillan Books for Africa, 1973), p. xii.

20.   Andrew Gurr, *Writers in Exile: The Creative Use of Home in Modern Literature* (Atlantic Highlands, N. J.: Humanities Press, 1981), p. 99.

21.   *Africa's Cultural Revolution*, p. 42.

Petals of Blood as a Popular Novel

Ngugi wa Thiong'o's *Petals of Blood* has already been hailed as one of the most significant novels to be published in Africa in the Seventies. Numerous copies have been sold all over the world, book reviewers and literary critics have lavished pages of commentary on it, and at least two international conferences – one in France, the other in California – have had sessions devoted to explication and analysis of its artistic and ideological features. Such rapid recognition, particularly from scholars, is unusual for a literary work that has been in print only a few years. *Petals of Blood* shows every sign of becoming an instant classic.

One event that undoubtedly contributed to the novel's notoriety was the imprisonment of its author six months after publication. Ngugi was hauled in for questioning by Kenyan police authorities on December 31, 1977, and was not released until nearly a year later. Since no formal charges were ever filed against him, it is impossible to say with any assurance whether the publication of *Petals of Blood* had anything to do with his detention, as some early reports in the Western press surmised it might.[1] In retrospect it appears that another of his literary and cultural activities, the co-authoring of a highly political musical drama in Gikuyu that was performed by villagers at the Kamirithu Community Educational and Cultural Centre in Limuru from October through November of 1977, may have been more directly responsible for his incarceration,[2] but *Petals of Blood*, if not the very last straw, must have added uncomfortable pressure to the government's spine. Certainly, during the following year, Ngugi's well-publicized plight as a political detainee drew attention to the novel, keeping it in the public eye and arousing international curiosity about constraints on freedom of expression in Kenya. *Petals of Blood*, though never censored or banned, was perceived as a courageously frank book that got its outspoken author into trouble with a repressive regime. Ngugi was being martyred for speaking his mind.

Yet even without such sensational publicity, the novel probably would have made its mark in a relatively short period of time. Ngugi was regarded as Kenya's leading novelist, and he had not published a major work of fiction since 1967. He had kept himself busy in the intervening decade with other projects – a book of literary and cultural essays, a collection of his short stories, a reorganization of the University of Nairobi's English Department into a Department of Literature that placed

African oral and written literatures at the heart of the curriculum[3] – but it was known that he was working on another blockbuster, and many of his fans were impatient to read it. A crisis would not have been necessary to increase public awareness of a new novel by Ngugi.

But ever since publication of *Petals of Blood*, questions have been raised about its adequacy as a work of fiction. Some critics have felt that Ngugi's techniques are far too bluntly didactic to be aesthetically pleasing, that politics impoverishes his art, ultimately rendering it nugatory. In other words, this novel fails because the author's ever-explicit commitment cripples and constrains his imagination. C. B. Robson, for example, in an otherwise positive assessment of the new complexities Ngugi introduces into his fiction in this work, finds

> Ngugi's characterisation in *Petals of Blood* is not as successful as in his earlier novels...The basic fault throughout is that features of character are imposed. They neither emerge nor evolve naturally from behaviour and interaction. We are told certain facts about the major characters but their actions do not generate sufficient emotional conviction to maintain them as valid creations.[4]

Robson attributes this kind of failure to the urgency underlying Ngugi's attempt to communicate his message:

> In *Petals of Blood* Ngugi goes beyond what is acceptable in fiction; he is giving us polemic. Basically it is a question of balance, and Ngugi's concern that we should not miss a detail sometimes results in a dominating and intrusive authorial presence...Indeed, both plot and character sometimes become simply devices to enable Ngugi to make his point.[5]

Eustace Palmer, while similarly impressed with Ngugi's progress as a novelist and his ambition to present "the most comprehensive analysis so far of the evils perpetrated in independent African society by black imperialism," confesses to having

> an uneasy feeling that Ngugi has been too ambitious, that he has attempted to do too much within the compass of a single novel...Such a work is bound to be uneven in quality. There are brilliant scenes, superbly realized, alternating at times with rather more tedious ones.[6]

Palmer agrees with Robson that

> This is partly due to the fact that Ngugi's chosen method of narration – the use of reminiscences – involves much more telling than showing. There seems to be a preponderance of narration and assertion over detailed scenic demonstration.[7]

Palmer also finds Ngugi's unstable characterization, particularly of a weak "hero" such as Munira, rather unconvincing: "The art here seems much cruder than that we have come to associate with Ngugi."[8]

Even two recent radical appraisals of *Petals of Blood* – a Marxist analysis by Ntongela Masilela and a socialist critique by Jürgen Martini – admit impediments to the true marriage of Ngugi's art and politics. Masilela feels that this

> admirable and significant novel is somewhat marred by Ngugi wa Thiong'o's tendency of forcing into the narrative texture of real historical events, situations and happenings which are not imaginatively and organically integrated or incorporated into the narrative structure of the novel.[9]

Martini is even more emphatic:

> Ngugi's novel is both realistic and utopian – the novel gives an important analysis of the reality in a developing capitalist country, but confronts this reality with a utopian wish for a better society. Whenever he introduces this utopian feature into the novel the writing becomes sentimental and downright bad. This is a way of thinking about society and a stylistic incompetence which Ngugi shares with other utopian writers...Whereas most of Ngugi's other novels end on a pessimistic note, *Petals of Blood* tries to be optimistic but by doing so destroys most of the argument of the novel and most of its stylistic coherence...In trying to avoid pessimism Ngugi neglects the results of his own analysis and introduces an utopian element that because it is so completely separated from reality cannot be regarded as a feasible alternative and is nothing else but wishful thinking.[10]

Poor characterization, unacceptable polemics, intrusive authorial presence, overambitious scope, uneven quality, forced imaginative integration, stylistic incompetence, sentimental optimism, utopian wishful thinking – on hearing such epithets, one begins to wonder whether *Petals of Blood* really merits being called a contemporary classic. It evidently has not impressed every reader; even those predisposed toward praising its strengths have noted a number of debilitating weaknesses. Judging from these critiques, it is far from a flawless piece of fiction. Ngugi may have his heart in the right place, but the critical consensus seems to be that he does not always have his art where it should be. Perhaps ideology and art are such strange bedfellows that the offspring of their union is bound to be somewhat coarse, wild, unbalanced or morphologically deformed.

Naturally, this assumption is based on elitist critical criteria that value form over content, style over substance, manner over matter. Literary critics concerned principally with aesthetics are likely to be disappointed with a work that sets out mainly to preach a message. But for Ngugi, truth is more important than beauty, so the message takes priority over the medium. Ngugi himself, in a speech delivered in 1974, while he was in a middle of writing *Petals of Blood*, stated that he refused to go along with the general tendency

> to see literature as something belonging to a surreal world, or to a metaphysical ethereal plane, something that has nothing to do with man's more mundane, prosaic realm of attempting to clothe, shelter and feed himself.[11]

He went on to say that

> A writer after all comes from a particular class and race and nation...A writer is trying to persuade us, to make us view not only a certain kind of reality, but also from a certain angle of vision often, though perhaps unconsciously, on behalf of a certain class, race, or nation...Seen in this light, the product of a writer's pen both reflects reality and also attempts to persuade us to take a certain attitude to that reality. The persuasion can be a direct appeal on behalf of a writer's open doctrine or it can be an indirect appeal through "influencing the imagination, feelings and actions of the recipient" in a certain way towards certain goals and a set of values, consciously or unconsciously held by him.[12]

So in response to critics who claim that not all propaganda is art, Ngugi would insist that all art, whether artists are aware of it or not, is propaganda.

Perhaps, then, the best method for evaluating *Petals of Blood* is to dispense with formalistic qualitative considerations and concentrate on the novel as a conduit of ideas and images meant to shape social attitudes. For instance, one could attempt to devise a reliable quantitative instrument to measure the impact of the book in Kenya and elsewhere; this could conceivably take the form of an opinion poll based on a random sample of readers' reactions, or a carefully controlled experiment to determine whether readers' political perceptions are in fact modified significantly after exposure to this novel, or even an armchair statistical analysis of the number and geographical distribution of copies sold at home and abroad. But all this objective data, useful though it might be in supporting or demolishing competing claims about the contemporary significance of *Petals of Blood*, would not help us to answer the biggest question of all concerning any literary work: Will it endure? Is it of lasting significance?

My answer to this ultimate, crystal-ball question is yes, it will. I believe that *Petals of Blood* will be around for a long time to come and will be read by many generations of Africans and non-Africans with pleasure and profit. But I base this belief on neither the politics nor the poetics of Ngugi's prose. Rather, I believe that *Petals of Blood* will survive because it is in essence a popular novel.

By this I do not mean to suggest that it is a potboiler written for mass consumption and maximum financial profit. Nor do I wish to imply that it is an inferior work of art jerry-built from a scrapheap of tired formulas, conventions and cliches. *Petals of Blood* is an original piece of fiction which addresses important social issues in a responsible fashion. It should be recognized and appreciated as serious, not trivial, literature.

Yet it justifiably may be termed "popular" because it appeals to deep human emotions in a forthright manner by portraying highly dramatic events emblematic of elemental struggles between good and evil. Whatever else may be said about *Petals of Blood*, it definitely is not a subtle, enigmatic work riddled with ambiguities and elusive symbols. The fundamental oppositions are always clear: angels wrestle with devils, and after a series of unjust setbacks, begin to emerge victorious from the struggle. At the end of the novel, paradise lost promises to give way to paradise regained. This utopian ending is not a defect in the narrative but rather a normal extension of the inexorable logic of any religious literature. For unless long-suffering saints are finally rewarded for their pains, what is the point of keeping the faith? One might as well sell out, join the sinners, and enjoy life.

All the major sinners in *Petals of Blood* are demons incapable of changing their base nature. They have insatiable appetites and fasten themselves parasitically on the healthier members of society whose life-blood they drink. Chui, Mzigo, Kimeria, Nderi wa Riera, Rev. Jerrod Brown, and such lackeys as Insect and Fat Stomach represent the exploitative upper class of politicians, bureaucrats, landowners, entrepreneurs, religious leaders and their hangers-on – a class of loathsome creatures equated with cannibals, vampires, leeches, jiggers and bedbugs. All these bloodsuckers and their authoritarian European counterparts – Rev. Hallowes Ironmonger, Cambridge Fraudsham, Sir Swallow Bloodall – are denounced throughout the novel as oppressors obsessed with power, privilege and position, monsters spawned by an inherently corrupt economic system that thrives on injustice and inequality.

The innocent victims in this schematic melodrama are the little people in the society – shopkeepers, primary school teachers, laborers, farmers, barmaids, prostitutes – the class of people Ngugi refers to in many of his essays as "peasants and workers."[13] Abdulla, Munira, Karega and Wanja are the principal representatives of this group but they are supported by a cast of thousands. These proletarian heroes and heroines are not wholly admirable characters, for nearly all of them have been bent out of shape by the harsh pressures of the world in which they live. They have had to compromise their integrity in some way in order to survive or they have yielded to gaudy temptations they ought to have resisted. Our sympathies are with them because they are poor, oppressed and frail, yet they possess enormous courage and resilience. They endure their hardships bravely, buckling only when they are intolerably overburdened or victimized by brutal tyrannical forces. But even their defeats may lead to moral victories. When Wanja feels compelled to resume her career as a prostitute, she does not lose her human dignity. Indeed, her relapse enables her to wreak revenge on the man who had ruined her life. The little people, Ngugi assures us, finally will win.

But to change their world, the oppressed proletariat will have to change their ways, uniting in the struggle against their oppressors. The novel documents how one community, on becoming aware of the extent to which they were being exploited, took matters into their own hands and started a revolution. They succeeded primarily because they ventured to challenge authority collectively. The moral of the story is that the meek shall inherit the earth only after they band together and shed their meekness. This requires that they form a new perception of themselves, recognizing their ability to shape their own destiny. Through enlightened community action comes true freedom.

Petals of Blood thus pits pure demons against besmirched peasants and workers who ultimately sweat their way into heaven. The demons never change, but the proletarian pilgrims do by becoming conscious of their chains and struggling to remove them. The story is an epic contest between alert commitment and supine obliviousness, between the morally quick and the morally dead. By making us aware of what is at stake in this very real yet highly symbolic battle, *Petals of Blood* serves as a bible of postcolonial social activism, reflecting and projecting the "correct" course of the modern African revolution. The novel itself, an instructive schematized paradigm of reality, heightens the political consciousness of the reader.

But even while educating us, this paradigmatic parable remains a popular novel grounded in a narrative tradition that is instantly recognizable. The tale begins as a whodunit, an ordinary murder mystery. Suspects are being rounded up for questioning after three pillars of the community – Mzigo, Chui and Kimeria – have been burnt to death one night in a brothel in Ilmorog. The suspects – Munira, Abdulla, Karega and Wanja – reminisce about the past and it soon becomes clear from their recollections that any or all of them could be guilty; certainly each had a valid motive for killing one or more of the victims. The job of Inspector Godfrey, an African Sherlock Holmes, is to piece together the evidence like a jigsaw puzzle and determine who set the fire.

However, as one scrap of personal history is added to another, the picture that emerges in the reader's mind is rather different from the one Inspector Godfrey is gradually assembling. It becomes apparent that the real culprits, the real mass murderers, are the victims themselves. These bourgeois parasites deserved ignominious death because they had spent their lives oppressing and exploiting their people. Once the full story is told, the true solution to the murder mystery turns out to be a surprising paradox: the actual murderers, Munira and Wanja, are innocent and so are the other suspects, for the dead victims are guilty of their own undoing. Capitalism is whodunit, and capitalism itself must die.

Like all successful popular literature, *Petals of Blood* has great mythopoeic power. It presents ideas and images which are invested with a compelling logic of their own, forcing us imaginatively to transcend everyday realities. The process of reading such works enables us to see a portion of the world anew and thus to revaluate our complacent assumptions about what is and what should be. This hallucinatory experience can yield great psychological satisfaction, awakening in us an impulse to dream more boldly, unconstrained by mundane facts.

Leslie Fiedler, commenting on the therapeutic function of all literature but particularly of popular literature, said it

> always carries on an underground war, out of sight but not out of mind, not out of our deep mind: a war against all the values professed by all conformist defenders of whatever reigning culture; against spirit, against civilization, against self-control, against rationality, against sanity, against law and order.[14]

Petals of Blood, by offering readers this kind of psychologically liberating experience, is a subversive work in the best sense of the word. It reshapes our thoughts and kindles our imagination, encouraging us to go beyond the here and now and actively contemplate new possibilities for the future. This may be the major reason why, despite the complaints of its detractors, *Petals of Blood*, Africa's first proletarian popular novel, is likely to outlive us all.

NOTES

1. See, e.g., Charles R. Larson, "African Dissenters," *New York Times Book Review*, 19 February 1978, pp. 3, 22.

2. See, e.g., Ahmed Rajab, "Detained in Kenya," *Index on Censorship*, 7, 3 (1978), 7-10.

3. *Homecoming: Essays on African and Caribbean Literature, Culture and Politics* (London: Heinemann, 1972); *Secret Lives* (London: Heinemann, 1975); Ngugi discusses reorganizing literature study at the University of Nairobi in "On the Abolition of the English Department," *Homecoming*, pp. 145-50.

4. C. B. Robson, *Ngugi wa Thiong'o* (New York: St. Martin's Press, 1979), pp. 99-100.

5. *Ibid.*, pp. 101-02.

6. Eustace Palmer, "Ngugi's *Petals of Blood*," *African Literature Today*, 10 (1979), 153, 165. Palmer reprints this essay in his book, *The Growth of the African Novel* (London: Heinemann, 1979), pp. 288-306.

7. *Ibid.*, p. 16.

8. *Ibid.*, p. 160.

9. Ntongela Masilela, "Ngugi wa Thiong'o's *Petals of Blood*," *Ufahamu*, 9, 2 (1979), 23.

10. Jürgen Martini, "Ngugi wa Thiong'o: East African Novelist," in *Individual and Community in Commonwealth Literature*, ed. Daniel Massa (Msida, Malta: University of Malta Press, 1979), p. 10.

11. Ngugi wa Thiong'o, "Literature and Society," *Writers in Politics* (London: Heinemann, 1981), p. 6. This essay earlier appeared in the proceedings of an African literature conference held in Nairobi in 1974, *Teaching of African Literature in Schools*, ed. Eddah Gachukia and S. Kichamu Akivaga (Nairobi: Kenya Literature Bureau, 1978), pp. 1-29.

12. *Ibid.*, pp. 6-7. Ngugi quotes from Arnold Hauser in this passage.

13. See, e.g., the address he gave when *Petals of Blood* was launched in Nairobi: "Petals of Love," *Writers in Politics*, pp. 94-98.

14. Leslie Fiedler, "Giving the Devil His Due," *Journal of Popular Culture*, 12 (1978), 207.

The New David Maillu

In the 1970s David Maillu emerged as the most significant popular writer in Kenya. This he accomplished not by writing school books for local branches of international publishing houses nor by soliciting the patronage of government-subsidized Kenyan publishers but by establishing his own firm, Comb Books, and inundating the market with novelettes and volumes of verse he himself had written, published, and then energetically promoted. His first "mini-novel," *Unfit for Human Consumption* (1973), the costs of which had been underwritten partly by a loan from a friend and partly by a trade agreement with a distributor, had sold so well that he had been able to invest the proceeds in a second book, *My Dear Bottle* (1973), a poetic apostrophe to the consolations of inebriation. This too had been swallowed up quickly by a pop-thirsty reading public, and Maillu had plowed the profits back into the firm just as quickly, bringing out in the next year another mini-novel, *Troubles* (1974), and another humorous soliloquy in verse, *After 4:30* (1974), as well as reissuing the first two sold-out titles. By repeating this kind of pyramiding procedure, Maillu in four years was able to publish twelve books he himself had written (including a Swahili translation of *My Dear Bottle*), reprint the best-selling works several times, and publish four books by other Kenyan authors who had similar stories to tell. By the middle of 1976 Comb Books had expanded to a staff of seven or eight fulltime employees occupying two stories of an office building in downtown Nairobi, and nearly all the technical aspects of book production – from type-setting on modern IBM machinery to designing of multi-colored jackets – were being handled in-house. Maillu made such an impact on the East African book world that other publishers rushed to emulate his example, introducing their own series of romantic novelettes and long-winded lyrical ruminations, often with photographs or drawings of sexy-looking girls on the covers. It was clear from this frantic competition that Comb Books had been a hair-raising success.

But Maillu's fortunes changed rather abruptly in 1976. First, in June that year, his books were banned in Tanzania, so he lost his major "foreign" market to the south. Political instability in Ethiopia and economic chaos in Uganda under Idi Amin had already robbed him of export opportunities on other borders, so just as his publishing house was beginning to grow and expand, the potential market for his books was contracting. However, by this time, encouraged by his early successes, he was printing a minimum of ten thousand copies of each new book he wrote, and his reprint runs sometimes went as high as thirty thousand copies. Eventually he overextended himself, and the pyramid came crashing down. He published no books in 1977, and the only titles to appear under the Comb Books imprint in 1978 were *English Punctuation* and *English Spelling and Words Frequently Confused*, which he had put together under the pseudonym of Vigad G. Mulila. His creditors sued him, forced him into bankruptcy, closed down his Nairobi office, and seized his business property, auctioning it off in September 1978 to pay a portion of the 700,000 shillings (about $100,000) he still owed them. Comb Books, a bold experiment in popular publishing, thus died in its sixth year.

But Maillu has not remained silent since then. Under a new imprint, David Maillu Publishers Ltd., he has brought out three new books of his own and has reissued a 1975 Comb Books title he supposedly co-authored with a prostitute. He has also published three novels in the Macmillan Pacesetters series, has a third in press, and he has a very long fourth novel (ca. 600-720 pages) completed and under consideration in London. In addition, he has finished a novelette that he hopes will help to raise "a few million shillings" for the Koola Town Self-Help and Community Development Scheme near his hometown of Machakos; he has invited Kenya's President Daniel arap Moi to write a foreword for this book. Maillu reports that he is currently busy writing an epic of Akamba life covering the period from 1781 to 1981, a volume that might turn out to be twice as long as the most ambitious work he has attempted so far.[1] The author who began his literary career with popular mini-novels in 1973 was thus turning his hand to giant blockbusters eight years later.

What happens to a writer's work when he can no longer publish all of his own books and therefore must submit some of his manuscripts to a foreign publisher? What happens to his work when harsh economic realities force him to choose very carefully what he himself is going to risk scarce capital to publish? What happens, in other words, when a totally free creative spirit is placed under constraints he has never before experienced? Does he express himself in a different way? Does he deal with different themes, different situations, different characters, different ideas? Or does he resort to the familiar formulas that have won him his reputation, seeking thereby to repeat earlier successes? David Maillu, a self-made literary phenomenon who went from pop to bust and is now trying to float a second career balloon is rough weather, provides an interesting case study of the popular artist under pressure. What strategies has he employed to survive?

When Maillu first appeared on the East African literary scene, he introduced an innovation that no other writer in his part of the world had exploited so fully: he talked dirty. True, Charles Mangua had done this a little earlier in Kenya in two extremely popular novels, *Son of Woman* (1971) and *A Tail in the Mouth* (1972), but Mangua wrote humorous picaresque tales in which a street-wise hero talked tough and dirty. Maillu may have learned something from Mangua, but his own civil servant heroes were not roughshod rogues but middle-class victims of biological urges that ultimately destroyed their careers; they talked weak and dirty. For instance, here is the way *Unfit for Human Consumption* begins:

> Jonathan Kinama, civil servant in the Republic of Kenya, waited in the bank, at the counter, teller No. 2. His insides burnt with impatience, much impatience, for his two months salary. It was pay day, the end of the month April 1972. The bank was full of customers, men and women, and at such a time one had to wait for a very long time. The bank had assumed a strange smell, a blend of cigarette smoke, and cheap and expensive local and exotic perfumes. And there was a smell of sex, especially from some of the women who had come to the bank hurrying through the hot morning. However, such sex smell could only be detected by some experts like Jonathan Kinama who had great experience in women. There were women of all sizes, from the tallest to the shortest; from the most beautiful to the ugliest.
>
> Kinama decided to keep himself busy while waiting by looking at the women. There were many pretty women to entertain him, most of them modern looking, impressively smart with straightened hair, some wearing Afro-American wigs. All of them carried expensive handbags of cheetah skin, zebra, lion and plastic. This was the scene of the modern African woman. Kinama's eyes rested on one girl, yes, that one – a fat girl armed with huge breasts, and highly pronounced buttocks, obviously soft and comfortable, luxurious. There was something more of great interest about her. Her legs. Thickly set legs, beautiful of course, and enthusiastically polished by nature in chocolate brown. And she protected them in the latest fashion of ckings. A bird that fitted too well in her mini dress, a mahogany mini which matched very well with her body. Kinama calculated in his mind and passed her as a sexy bird.
>
> Her eyes met his and he quickly looked away pretending that he had not been looking at her. But not before he had managed to have a glance at her lips: full lips which seduced his for a kiss. He licked his lips. She was unaware that he had been studying her. Now she fell into conversation with a thin girl, nail-hard looking. They talked in English and the accent which came from the thin girl sounded doubtfully local. He studied the thin girl and found himself thinking, "How would a man hold this one?" But his eyes went back to the fat one in spite of the attractive accent of the thin one which was putting more value in her. Kinama's ideal girl for sex satisfaction and romance was a plump girl with shoulders that arched nicely and intoxicating breasts like those ones. He could hardly take his eyes from her. He waded through the crowd till he came to a

good position where he could see her face well. "Hi!" he thought, then he sighed.

"Man, this one," he thought, "this one is very much fit for human consumption!" He began wondering what man on earth enjoyed her.

"Delicious!" he thought and began surveying her legs, then her hips and..."Just there!" He thought and his penis began rising. (pp. 5-7)

Kinama, a middle-class tragic hero, does not rise very high before he suffers a middle-class fall, losing his job because he cannot control his desire for sex and alcohol. Distraught, he commits suicide.

It was this kind of story – the soap opera of civil servant self-destruction – that Maillu made his own in his first mini-novels and long poems. Sometimes he would focus on men, sometimes on women (usually working women – secretaries, schoolgirls, prostitutes and the like), but his stories seldom ended happily. The protagonist would have to suffer for having overindulged in the fleeting pleasures of the bed or bottle, pleasures which Maillu paused to describe in elaborate and zesty detail. Some of his detractors called such writing pornography, but it would be classified as rather innocuous softcore material on the bookshelves of any Western drugstore or supermarket, including those in Nairobi. Yet in East Africa no one before Maillu had written about such matters in quite the same way, with so much attention focused on the physiological and psychological dimensions of erotic and dipsomaniac behavior. It was no doubt this unusual "frankness," as Maillu terms it,[2] that won him so many readers. He talked dirty in a new way.

If we compare Maillu's latest works with those he wrote and published during Comb Books' brief heyday, one change becomes apparent immediately: the dirty talk is gone. His heroes may be sexually active but they are not sexually obsessed, and their physical interactions with members of the opposite sex tend to be described with restraint, even reticence. This is true not only in the two novels he has published in the Macmillan Pacesetter Series, *For Mbatha and Rabeka* (1980) and *The Equatorial Assignment* (1980), but also in *Kadosa* (1979), the first novel brought out by David G. Maillu Publishers Ltd., and in "Tears at Sunset," the yet unpublished novel written for the Koola Town Self-Help and Community Development Scheme. Moreover, carnal love has no place in *Jese Kristo* (1979), a morality play performed at the Kenya National Theatre in October and November of 1979 and published in the program prepared for that production, or in *Hit of Love* (1980), a one-hundred page poem issued by David Maillu Publishers Ltd. in a bilingual (English-Kikamba) format. The only exception or throwback to Maillu's earlier sexy style of writing is *The Flesh: Part One* (1979), a poem about prostitution purportedly written in

Kikamba by Jasinta Mote and translated, edited, "produced", and reprinted by Maillu after having been originally published by Comb Books in 1975. Since *The Flesh: Part One* belongs to an earlier phase in Maillu's career and may have been composed to some degree by someone else, it will not be considered here except as an example of what is produced by a hard-pressed softcore publisher returning to old tricks of the trade. Perhaps Maillu needed a proven bread-and-butter (or bed-and-better) title to get his new publishing venture off the ground. His previous experience in the popular book business would have taught him that prostitution sells.

But such pandering to prurient interests was not the sort of thing that an established British publisher would likely be eager to include in its own popular series. Every Macmillan Pacesetter contains the following policy statement: "All the novels in the Macmillan *Pacesetter* series deal with contemporary issues and problems in a way that is particularly designed to interest young adults, although the stories are such that they will appeal to all ages." The initial titles in the series are indicative of the pace Macmillan hoped to set: *The Smugglers, The Delinquent, The Betrayer, The Hopeful Lovers, Bloodbath at Lobster Close.* Clearly the emphasis was meant to be on formulaic fiction – stories of mystery, adventure, and romance. Young adults interested primarily in raw sex would have to seek their literary thrills elsewhere.

Maillu's success in adapting to new popular formulas is evident in the first two Pacesetters he has written. *For Mbatha and Rabeka* is built on a classic love triangle. Mbatha, an idealistic primary school teacher, is planning to marry Rabeka, his beautiful childhood sweetheart who teaches at the same village school. But while she is in Nairobi recovering from a liver ailment, she meets Honeycomb Mawa, a Panel Beater Foreman with Bodyliners Limited, who shows her the town in his Saab sportscar, wining and dining her at all the top establishments in the Rift Valley and escorting her to high-class international parties. Rabeka, dazzled by the urban glitter and impressed by Mawa's sophistication and wealth, begins to long for life in the fast lane:

> As soon as she returned to Kilindi, she noticed how primitive things were and how many essentials of living were missing. To start with, she saw how poor life was in the country. Then the list continued: there were no entertainment centres, no television, no high class hotels, no cinemas, no good transport facilities, no hairdressers, no newspapers, no bookshops or libraries, no intellectual with whom to discuss serious subjects, not to mention how far this place was from the city of international communication. (p. 99)

Mbatha, distressed by Rabeka's new materialistic outlook and heartbroken when she leaves him with the intention of marrying Mawa, has a mental breakdown that puts him in an asylum for six weeks. But the story ends happily when Mawa, unable to raise a substantial loan to cover his marriage expenses, fails to turn up for his own wedding, and Rabeka, embarrassed and tired of waiting, agrees to run off that same afternoon with her dependable beau. Village virtue thus wins out over big-city flashiness.

The story moves rapidly, and several vividly sketched minor characters add humor and variety to a fairly conventional romantic plot. Maillu, in bringing his lovers together, does not omit erotic encounters entirely, but most of the heavy-breathing action takes place in bedrooms or riverbanks offstage. The most intimate scene described is one in which Rabeka and Mawa, forced to share a guestroom in her uncle's Nairobi apartment, huddle together at night under a single blanket in order to keep warm. Unable to sleep, they leave the light on and talk for a while:

> Later, sleep overcame her and she blotted out, leaving him still brightly awake. He turned slowly and faced her in that semi-back position she lay. He studied her calm face that had now been taken over by the innocence of sleep. Her kissable lips lay loosely, very tempting...he felt her clear clean breath gently breezing over his face. He liked the way she breathed; he admired her nose, her eyelashes, that chin, those cheeks, all of which were given a fine finish by the pretty mouth – those lips again. Between her lips, her milk-white teeth half-showed...She smelt nice. He brought his mouth closely to hers, so that she breathed straight into his nostrils, not a stinking breath, but a living one; one though not fresh was refreshing, challenging, feminine. Slowly, he placed his arm over her bosom, doing his best not to awaken her. His hand lay just below her breasts.
>
> "Your highness," he called much, much later.
>
> "Yes," her eyes flew open, being sensitive to the light.
>
> "I can't sleep."
>
> "I'm sorry, I can't keep awake much more...What can I do for you to make you sleep for a while before we wake up?" She felt his hand across her bosom and didn't object.
>
> "I guess nothing you can do."
>
> "Put off the light and try to sleep, please."
>
> He reached the switch and put off the light then returned the hand back. She turned her back to him, took his hand and put it under her arm and, how daring! now put it over her breast as if she thought that was the only favour she could extend to him. "Please, for my sake, try to sleep."
>
> And he *did* sleep, though after a long time. (pp. 78-79)

The difference between the Pacesetter Maillu and the earlier sex-pacer Maillu is quite clear if we compare this kind of titillation with what comes to hand in any Comb Book. Here, for example, is an excerpt from *Troubles* in which a secretary, trying to win a promotion, meets her boss after hours in the office to feed him fish and chips and, in the process, arouse another of his appetites:

> He looked at her greedily as if she was a piece of nicely roasted chicken which he wanted to eat. Ema took everything easily, advancing by degrees. If things went on the way they looked, she thought, then she knew that she was on the right path to promotion. He began kneading her breasts and her eyes began responding. He kissed her lips, pulling her more to himself. They looked at each other, smiled, then when he kissed her this time, she gave him all her long tongue to suck on. He did it passionately, eating all the bits of chips on the tongue. She writhed in his hands. When he released her a little bit, she folded up the paper and put aside the chips, then pushed all her breasts to him. And he knew what to do with them...He kissed and sucked on her firm breasts, shattering her and triggering off her vagina powerfully excited and making it begin chewing its lips and trying to swallow them. He took a glance at the gloss black hair thatching her vagina.
>
> "Ohooo, Ohooo, Oho-o!" She cried as his pole drove into her lively flesh. She arched her hips up and up to meet him, hastening his powerful warm thing into a full swallow – complete homecoming...He knew too well how to drive a woman mad with it, building her up into a crushing climax. Now he took to another style, sucking and twirling his nipples. That amplified her crying, sometimes her breath locking up and storming out. Now he added his finger to twirling her clitoris. She squirmed, twisted, scratched the floor, and hit his legs with her heels. And when he began racing for the finals, she joined with a savage reaction and a saxophone note leaped her anus. Her orgasm spun to the gate synchronizing with his. Maiko began puffing out like a monster and just before they reached their climax, the telephone rang! But they hastened, punching each other wildly until the climax outbroke stormingly. (pp.112-17)

One doubts that a publisher such as Macmillan would have allowed its offices to be used to promote such creative works.

Maillu's second Pacesetter, *The Equatorial Assignment*, was an African adaptation of the James Hadley Chase type of thriller. Benni Kamba, Secret Agent 009 working for the National Integrity Service of Africa (NISA), is pitted against beautiful Konolulu, known professionally as Colonel Swipta, an agent for a multinational European organization intent on destabilizing Africa for the benefit of the Big Powers. NISA has its headquarters at a Saharan desert outpost run by the brainy Dr. Triplo, and Colonel Swipta works at a mountain station called Chengolama Base run by the unscrupulous and equally brilliant Dr. Thunder. Benni Kamba's mission is to infiltrate Chengolama Base and destroy it before Dr. Thunder can launch his secret weapon, a missle called Thundercrust that would obliterate NISA. Agent 009 accomplishes this by making romantic overtures to Colonel

Swipta, killing her after gaining her trust, and then detonating the Thundercrust on its launching pad, thereby destroying Chengolama Base. The good guys win; the bad guys die.

The action-packed plot of this adventure story includes a kidnapping, a high-speed car chase, an assassination attempt, a submarine maneuver, a spying mission, a helicopter getaway, an airplane pursuit, several dastardly betrayals, and countless explosions and murders. Moreover, it is all good, clean fun, with cunning and courage triumphing over might and malice. The earthiest episodes, Benni Kamba's few tumbles with Konolulu, are handled playfully rather than pornographically:

> They spent the night together in Kamba's flat. Very early the next morning, they swam far out to sea together. Obviously this girl was a powerful swimmer, too.
>
> As they swam round each other, rising and falling with the waves, Kamba thought she was funny in bed. He remembered the manner in which she had coiled and uncoiled, then made that single and final brief cry, "Jjjjaha!"...
> They swam closely.
> "You know what?" she said. "I'm swimming naked, come and feel me."
> He passed his hand over her breasts, then down there.
> "Beware of the small fish!" (pp. 34-35).

This is light fiction written with a light touch. Unlike *For Mbatha and Rabeka*, *The Equatorial Assignment* does not deal with semi-serious social issues or with real people in recognizable situations. It is escape literature pure and simple, and indigenous variant of an extremely popular foreign genre. Benni Kamba is an African James Bond.

The books Maillu himself has published in recent years are no saltier than those he has published with Macmillan, but they tend to reflect other facets of his personality as a writer. In the play *Jese Kristo* he sets the story of Jesus Christ is a modern African state, the Republic of Savannah, in order to explore a number of related political and theological notions. The historical analogy enables him to comment on injustice, tyranny, violence, and the persecution of innocent and upright people in contemporary Africa in a dramatic context that his audience could not fail to understand. This is satire with provocative symbolic punch.

In the bilingual poem *Hit of Love*, Maillu meditates on the nature of love, asking such questions as "Why do I live at all, and for what?" "Does love find or is love found?" "Do I love you or am I made to love you?" "Does love regret?" "Can love be counted in terms of profits and gains?" "Who is responsible for what I feel?" "How do I fit in the solar system of your life?" This restless questioning is not unlike the compulsive talkativeness in some of his early long poems, especially the garrulous *The*

Kommon Man, which comes in three volumes and runs to nearly 850 pages. Maillu's keen interest in philosophy and "the moral side of life" achieves expression in this kind of contemplative verse.

A more pragmatic love problem is the theme of Maillu's unpublished community development novel, "Tears at Sunset." A beautiful young woman (with the unlikely name of Swastika Nzivele) has married a hardworking young man, Silvesta Maweu, whose family home is in the dry hill country of Kenya. Unfortunately, his work as a bank accountant keeps him far away at the coast most of the year, and Swastika is left upcountry with the responsibility not only of maintaining their homestead and farm but also of caring for his eighty-year-old mother, Kalunde. At first the two women get along well, but their relationship deteriorates when Kalunde criticizes Swastika for throwing a dinner party and dance one night during her husband's absence. Worse yet, Swastika takes up – and occasionally takes off – with a married neighbor, Simon Mosi, who owns a large farm across the river. When Silvesta returns home unexpectedly and finds her gone, he is furious, but his mother and the village pastor calm him down, and he and Swastika are reunited momentarily. However, as soon as he goes away again, Swastika backslides into unwifely behavior, seeing too much of Simon and too little of her ailing mother-in-law. She even poisons the family dog so he will not bark when Simon pays his evening visits. The next time Maweu comes home, he thrashes her soundly and threatens to kill her. She leaves and it appears that their marriage is broken, but he still loves her, misses her, and eventually tries to get her back. When Kalunde dies, Swastika returns to him and they live happily ever after in the highlands, raising three childlren and building up their farm by constructing a big dam and employing modern methods of irrigation. What had been dry and barren is cultivated at last and bears healthy fruit.

Maillu touches upon a number of topical matters in this story, not the least of which is the plight of the mateless married woman in rural society. Swastika's problem is that she feels bored and unfulfilled living alone upcountry. As she says in a long letter to Silvesta after their breakup,

> I think I just found myself very lonely, or afraid of myself, and I just got involved. Country life has many problems. A whole barren world in which you find yourself in no other company but that of village and little educated women. I am not trying to argue that I am better than they are; but it is that they and I belong to different worlds. You will probably think that I am talking a lot of nonsense.
>
> I think I have one great problem, call it weakness. I can't exist like that without doing anything. That is, I feel that I must engage myself or be occupied by something concrete. Not just trying to supervise some labourers digging coffee holes or making terraces. I need something more than that.

After your duty in Mombasa, you stroll around, doing some window-shopping or sight-seeing, or go for a swim or to watch the sea as I know you like doing, or see a movie. But what do I have in Kyandumbi or at Koola Town? I am sure I am not the only person seeing it that way. Until there are facilities in a place like that, you can expect worse things from younger people.

In the old days, people were kept busy by their social activities – dance, communal celebrations for circumcisions and childbirth, initiations, participation in clan affairs, looking after the livestock and large families, and so on. What have we today in that place?

Nothing, absolutely nothing.

And yet, one is expected to live there happily. It is a nice place, but it lacks other things. The desert looks very beautiful, with all those sand dunes, and so on, as you might have seen in films; but no one would like to live in it, because it lacks other factors that are essential to life. Of course, I am not trying to liken Koola to the desert, but I am sure you know what I am trying to say. The place doesn't lack water alone, but many other things. I would love to live in a place like that, in the country, if there were other things to occupy my mind.

I don't know whether you can connect this with my behavior. Had I been a teacher or something, maybe my time there would have been less boring. I didn't love that Mosi the way you thought. It was a problem deeper than that, and I have great doubt whether you will ever understand it. There is nothing I am trying to justify about the whole involvement. It goes without question that it was immoral behavior...That was also the cause of my disagreement with your mother. It would be good for me to simply say that I got messed up...A friend of mine once told me that even paradise would be boring without some form of occupation. (pp. 84-85 of unpublished typescript)

It is apparent from Swastika's astute effort at self-analysis that her problem is rather different from that of Rabeka in *For Mbatha and Rabeka*. She is not attracted by the gaudy tinsel of city life or the smooth talk of fast men. She simply needs a productive outlet for her energy, something intellectually engaging that will keep her stimulated and busy.

Maillu evidently perceives such environmentally induced ennui to be a major source of unhappiness and social disorder in contemporary Africa, for he returns to this theme again and again in his writings. In the introduction to *Jese Kristo* he remarks that

Most of the adults in Africa today are standing face to face with the devil of "having nothing to do after work, and having nothing for entertainment"...Most of the heavy drinking that is invading the country says that something is seriously wrong somewhere. When man lacks the means of recreation, he turns to drinking, sex, and crime...There is so much mental hunger in their country that one wonders what could be done to, at least, cut it down by fifty percent. In Western worlds, there are theatres, clubs, sports, dances, films, television, books, – the list is long – available to everyone. In our worlds, these are for a

few individuals, the élite. For the mass and the common man, there is the bottle
and the woman and the mouth. It is not surprising that our countries have the
highest birth rates in the world...The common man has hardly any chances of
educating himself beyond where the teacher left him. Food alone is not enough
to sustain the human life. (pp. 4, 16)

Maillu the moralist, Maillu the practical psychologist, Maillu the homespun
philosopher, Maillu the comedian, Maillu the popular publisher, tries to provide the kind of stimulating entertainment that will satisfy the mental hunger
of his people and thereby help to sustain the "human life" in Kenya.

Perhaps the most encouraging sign of Maillu's growth as a creative
artist has been his willingness to experiment with new forms and new ideas.
Instead of continuing to churn out only one type of literature, he has moved
in a number of different directions simultaneously, dabbling in drama as
well as fiction and poetry, and trying his hand at everything from spy
thrillers and domestic melodramas to religio-political satire and narrative
verse. But his most remarkable piece of writing since the demise of Comb
Books must certainly be the first book he published in the David Maillu
Publishers Library series launched in 1979, a novel called *Kadosa*, which the
author himself terms his "most favorite work."[3]

Kadosa is a blend of romance, adventure, science fiction, metaphysical
speculation, and hallucinogenic horror. It concerns a love affair between Dr.
Mutava, a scholar returning to Kenya to complete a study of "African
Mythology and Apparition," and a young mysterious supernatural creature
named Kadosa who is herself an apparition. Kadosa possesses immense
powers, including the ability to transform herself at will into anything visible
or invisible. She treats Mutava to terrifying displays of her total control over
the bodies and minds of human beings, injuring and even killing those who
annoy her. She also rules Mutava's imagination, filling his dreams and other
unconscious moments with horrific sights that nearly drive him mad. Mutava
calls in another scientist from Switzerland to study her, but the old professor
flees after Kadosa turns his head coal black. Mutava, despite all his qualms
and traumas, finds himself powerfully attracted to this phenomenal femme
fatale, and he is genuinely sorry when she ultimately is called back to another world. She leaves him pondering the illusory demarcation between
being and unbeing.

This was, in many senses, a fantastic way for Maillu to begin his second
literary career. *Kadosa* was utterly unlike anything he had written before. For
one thing, there was no sex in it; the love affair between Mutava and Kadosa
was absolutely platonic, with the primary point of focus throughout being on
marvels of fantasy rather than matters of physiology. *Kadosa* literally took the
reader to another world. The boldness of Maillu's conception may be sampled

in any of the uncanny nightmares that haunt this book. Here, for instance, is one of Dr. Mutava's hallucinations in a movie theatre:

> The screen flipped and instantly another scene came. Someone stood by a very large gate: he was dressed in white, but a red cap was on his head. A stethoscope hung around his neck. He wore red shoes. The walls of the house he was seen in faded out into a grey darkness and I could not see properly what was beyond the grey darkness. The door next to which this man stood was, like the gate, very wide. I looked carefully at him and came to the conclusion that he was a doctor...From his left, I saw a long line of women advancing towards the doctor. And on coming close to him, each bent, uncovered her bottom and the doctor pushed an injection into her quickly, then she passed. There were women of all sizes and of all races. The doctor acted very quickly on them, throwing glances here and there as if he were afraid of being seen by anyone. But just as soon as each patient passed the doctor, she began to wail and writhe in pain.
>
> That scene passed quickly and I saw the women come out from another opening into the building. And upon entering a large parlour, they dropped onto the floor and blood began to pour out from them as they wailed and writhed in pain. Some of them lay in the pools of blood as if they were dead. But on the left-hand side of the house, another person who looked like a doctor, but this time wearing a green cap and green shoes, stood there with a long knife and each time a pregnant woman passed by him, he stabbed her in the stomach and took out the child and while the child was still kicking in his hands, he threw it through a window and left blood-stains running down the wall. Then that woman would fall down immediately and she would wail and writhe in the agony of the pain like all the others. After this scene, the screen faded into something else: there was a big heap which, when I tried to find out what it was, I discovered that it was composed of dead babies, some still kicking with a bit of life in them, others who had only been a few months old before they were delivered...(pp. 60-61)

This vividly visualized horror is followed by other cinematographic sequences equally intense. Maillu, in delving so deeply into morbid zones of the imagination, was breaking new ground in African fiction. *Kadosa* was the first Kenyan novel to explore the surreal mysteries of the occult.

Literary critics have not been very generous in their assessment of Maillu's work. No one has lavished praise on him, and few have admitted finding any redeeming value in what or how he writes. The general feeling among serious academics appears to be that such literature is beneath criticism for it is wholly frivolous, the assumption being that a scholar should not waste his time on art that aims to be truly popular. Yet Maillu cannot be ignored in any systematic effort to understand the evolution of an East African literature, for he has extended the frontiers of that literature farther than any other single writer. One may regard his writing as undisciplined, unrefined, uncouth and outrageously excessive, but it is precisely because he has been spectacularly audacious and unmannerly that he is important. He has broken most of the rules of good writing and has gotten away with it, thereby releasing an embryonic literary culture from the confining sac of conformity to established conventions of taste and judgement. Maillu, a primitive pioneer and intrepid trailblazer, has liberated fenced-off aesthetic territory. Now that he has pushed the boundaries of decorum back, others can stake out their own claims in the same untamed wilderness.

Moreover, Maillu is important because he possesses tenacity and resourcefulness. He has learned to survive by adjusting to new circumstances and imposing his will on the world about him. He has taken risks that the prudent would have eschewed and has discovered through trial and error, as well as through trial and success, just how far he can carry others with him. One has to admire his courage both as a publisher and as an author. Perhaps no one else would have persisted so long in the struggle when buffeted continually by criticism that everything he produced was unfit for human consumption.

NOTES

1.   Letters from David Maillu to Bernth Lindfors dated 18 September 1981 and 14 December 1981.

2.   "Interview with David Maillu," *Mazungumzo: Interviews with East African Writers, Publishers, Editors and Scholars*, ed. Bernth Lindfors (Athens, Ohio: Ohio University Center for International Studies, African Program, 1980), p. 68.

3.   Written on title page of presentation copy of *Kadosa* given by David Maillu to Bernth Lindfors. In his letter of 14 December 1981, Maillu states that "*Kadosa* was conceived and partly written while I worked for Voice of Kenya, 1972" and "was going to appear in Comb Books list in 1977."

WORKS CITED

David G. Maillu. *Unfit for Human Consumption*. Nairobi: Comb Books, 1973.

. *My Dear Bottle*. Nairobi: Comb Books, 1973.

. *Troubles*. Nairobi: Comb Books, 1974.

. *After 4:30*. Nairobi: Comb Books, 1974.

. *The Kommon Man: Part One*. Nairobi: Comb Books, 1975.

. *The Kommon Man: Part Two*. Nairobi: Comb Books, 1975.

. *The Kommon Man: Part Three*. Nairobi: Comb Books, 1976.

. *No!* Nairobi: Comb Books, 1976.

. (pseud. Vigad G. Mulila) *English Spelling and Words Frequently Confused*. Nairobi: Comb Books, 1978.

. *Kadosa*. Machakos: David Maillu Publishers Ltd., 1979.

. *Jese Kristo*. Machakos: National Theatre Company and David Maillu Publishers Ltd., 1979.

. *For Mbatha and Rabeka*. London and Basingstoke: Macmillan, 1980.

. *The Equatorial Assignment*. London and Basingstoke: Macmillan, 1980.

. *Hit of Love: Wendo Ndikilo*. Machakos: David Maillu Publishers Ltd., 1980.

. "Tears at Sunset." Unpublished typescript.

Charles Mangua. *Son of Woman*. Nairobi: East African Publishing House, 1971.

. *A Tail in the Mouth*. Nairobi: East African Publishing House, 1972.

Jasinta Mote. ("Produced by David Maillu.") *The Flesh: Part One*. Nairobi: Comb Books, 1975; Machakos: David Maillu Publishers Ltd., 1979.

Popular Literature in Black South Africa

The popular literature of black South Africa that has been written in English may serve as a convenient example of how a new literature is shaped by environmental circumstances. Most black South Africans are not native speakers of English, and they acquire an ability to read and write this foreign "national" tongue only if they are fortunate enough to attend a school in which it is used as a medium of instruction. The white minority government of South Africa, for obvious political reasons, has been trying to hinder the spread of English among the black population by insisting that blacks learn in their own native languages, but those blacks who rise highest on the educational ladder as well as those who live in urban areas gain a functional command of English relatively early in life. These fortunate few have created nearly all the literature in English to have come out of black South Africa, and their efforts to reach their own people in a popular literary idiom have taken different forms at different times.

First it was fiction, a form generated by the appearance of the first pulp magazines in English for African readers. Although vernacular and English language newspapers aimed at a black reading public provided a creative outlet for black South African writers as early as the mid-nineteenth century and became important disseminators of information and opinion in the decade between the world wars,[1] it was not until much later that such printed media really began to reach a sizable audience. It was actually the establishment of *Drum* magazine in Johannesburg in 1951 that got a substantial black popular literature movement in English started in South Africa.[2] *Drum* was an enormously successful pictures-and-paragraphs pulp magazine that appealed to urban African readers not only in Johannesburg and Cape Town but in Accra, Lagos, Ibadan, Nairobi, Kampala, Dar es Salaam, Salisbury and other African cities as well. Indeed, so successful did it become that branch offices were soon set up in Ghana, Nigeria and Kenya to publish separate West and East African editions of the magazine. What made *Drum* so popular initially was a blend of flashy, muckraking journalism focusing on the injustices and indignities of apartheid and lively human interest reportage totally devoid of politics. Exposés of South African prison conditions or forced labor on Afrikaner farms ran side by side with feature articles on famous sports figures, jazz musicians, film stars and amusing eccentrics. Unusual murders, suicides, robberies, and rapes were described in vivid detail.

Pretty girls adorned the covers, and the back pages always contained a column offering frank advice to the lovelorn, another providing addresses and photographs of readers who wanted penpals, and numerous advertisements for skin lighteners, muscle and bust developers, blood tonics, and miscellaneous panaceas. In short, there was something in *Drum* for everyone.

The literary pages were usually filled with short fiction.[3] Occasionally these stories contained social or political protest, but more often they dripped with sentiment and sordid sensationalism. Anyone who could cram a memorable mixture of crime, violence and sex into a brief narrative stood a chance of winning *Drum*'s annual short story competition.[4] A typical offering, a gruesome tale entitled "Too Late to Love," describes a sailor taking revenge on the owner of a bar where he had been beaten and robbed after being picked up by a prostitute; here is an excerpt from the final barroom brawl:

> Boeta didn't know anything after that. A chain hook swung viciously up and down, found and lodged deep in his fat stomach, a ripping pull and his guts spilled all over the floor, his belly torn open. The scream welling up in his throat was stopped dead as a hand pike stabbed deep into his throat, a sort of coup de grace.[5]

A former editor of *Drum* once remarked that the "enormous majority" of stories submitted to the magazine "were fantasies of ferocity, centering either round gangster life in the townships or that legitimized outlet for violence – the boxing ring."[6]

Romantic love stories were next in order of frequency, a representative example being "Never Too Late for Love," which contains the following passage:

> Then she was in his arms, yielding to the warmth and passion of his kisses with a wild surrender she had never thought possible. The stars moved on in their heavenly orbits, throwing their warm, serene glow on trees, lengthening the shadows. [7]

This odd mixture of mayhem and saccharine tenderness dominated the literary pages of *Drum* until the late 1950s. *Drum*, of course, spawned a number of imitators that tried to cash in on its formula for commercial success. These new magazines augmented the demand for stories of blood and gore all over the floor and passionate kisses under the stars.[8]

There also arose a group of liberal, radical and communist serials that took a strong anti-apartheid line and encouraged African authors to write militant protest fiction. Publications such as *Fighting Talk, New Age, Africa South,* and *The New African* printed stories that revealed the frustrations, pains and indignities suffered by blacks in a white-ruled society. A typical story in *New Age* began:

> Monday morning was always the same: the police barging into houses, demanding passes from the men and pulling the houses upside down in search of beer.[9]

Another *New Age* story emphasizes the arbitrary injustice of the South African legal system:

> A man who had been ordered out of town built himself a house outside the borough, on his own piece of ground, out of his own savings. He was now being charged with occupying a house without a permit.[10]

The radical magazines and newspapers that published such stories provided an outlet for writers who wanted to change South African society, so a vigorous literature of political commitment grew up alongside the escapist literature in the pulp magazines. Some of South Africa's best known black writers – Ezekiel Mphahlele, Alex La Guma, Richard Rive, James Matthews, Bloke Modisane, Can Themba – got their start by contributing stories to one or both of these types of media.

Unfortunately, this short story writing movement was not destined to last very long. In 1963 it was brought to a halt by strict new censorship legislation in the form of a comprehensive Publications and Entertainments Act that threatened heavy penalties to publishers printing anything the courts might deem "indecent or obscene or offensive or harmful to public morals." Most of the liberal, radical and communist publications were banned, and some of the writers who had contributed to them were imprisoned or placed under house arrest. The pulp magazines cut down drastically on sex, violence and crime and began offering watered-down science fiction instead – something for which they were not likely to be taken to court.[11] During this period a number of black writers went into voluntary exile, leaving South Africa to live in Europe or other parts of the African continent. The short story movement which had flourished in the Fifties thus withered and died in the Sixties.

Then, in 1971, the silence that had settled over black South Africa was shattered by the publication of a book of poems entitled *Sounds of a Cowhide Drum* written by a messenger from Soweto named Oswald Joseph Mtshali. This extraordinary little book contained an unusual mixture of poignant personal reflections and sharp political observations. There was a strong element of protest in much of the verse, but the government censors were willing to let it pass, possibly because they regarded it as nothing serious – it was only poetry, after all. *Sounds of a Cowhide Drum* rapidly became a runaway best seller. More than ten thousand copies were sold in its first year, enough to persuade English and American publishers to hurry to bring out their own editions the following year.

One short poem called "Boy on a Swing" may help to convey the flavor of this volume:

> Slowly he moves
> to and fro, to and fro,
> then faster and faster
> he swishes up and down.
> His blue shirt
> billows in the breeze
> like a tattered kite.
>
> The world whirls by:
> east becomes west,
> north turns to south;
> the four cardinal points
> meet in his head.
>
> Mother!
> Where did I come from?
> When will I wear long trousers?
> Why was my father jailed?[12]

The effectiveness of this mode of political protest resides in its graphic simplicity and sudden climactic irony.

Mtshali's success encouraged other black poets to come forward. Mongane Wally Serote's *Yakhal'inkomo* and James Matthews's and Gladys Thomas's *Cry Rage!* appeared in 1972, anthologies of black South African poetry were brought out in 1973 and 1974, Sydney Sipho Sepamla's *Hurry up to it!* was issued in 1975, and Serote's second volume, *No Baby Must Weep*, came out in 1976.[13] The protest element in this new verse tended to be much louder and more blatant than in Mtshali's work. Here is a fairly typical poem by James Matthews from an anthology he edited called *Black Voices Shout!*:

living in our land is a political action
boarding a bus you see a sign that says
Black man, known your place
and Black woman even if you're 75
suffer from swollen limbs
you've got to climb those stairs
you cannot sit up front
living and dying is political
if you're Black
for your welfare they give you
slips of paper that turn living
into a nightmare and when dead they
extend their powers and shove you
into a hole in the ground allocated
away from them to remind you
of the way they forced you to live
and they say that the people
are a happy people, happy
in their separate boxes
not knowing that our smiles
are the masks we wear to cover
the rage that stirred up that will
jump out and tear white arrogance
apart for their political evils conjuring
our sunny land into a blazing hell[14]

This sudden eruption of popular political poetry would have been a very encouraging development in South African letters but for the fact that the censors soon started trying to suppress it. *Cry Rage!* and *Black Voices Shout!* were banned by the government, Matthews was arrested and imprisoned on August 31, 1976, presumably for his outspoken poetry, and Serote, after studying briefly in the United States, decided to go and live in Botswana rather than risk returning to South Africa. It is possible that this promising new poetry movement may be squashed out of existence the same way the short story movement was.

The one ray of hope in this rather bleak picture may be the Black South African theatre, which has been providing popular entertainment in African townships and suburbs since the 1950s. Not much has been known outside South Africa about these activities, though certain elaborate productions such as the musicals *King Kong* (in which Miriam Makeba starred in 1959) and *Sponono* (a 1963 show based on short stories by Alan Paton concerned with reformatory life) and later collaborative efforts of Athol Fugard, John Kani and Winston Ntshona in the plays *Sizwe Bansi is Dead, The Island*, and *Statements after an Arrest under the Immorality Act* have won international acclaim while touring the theatres of Europe and America. The township plays were of an entirely different order and magnitude. In Cape Town in the Fifties, groups of amateur actors with names like the Trafalgar Players, the Cameo Players, the Peninsula Dramatic Society, and the New Theatre used to get together to perform plays by Shaw, Genet, Brecht, and others in schools and community centers. They also sponsored play-writing competitions for high school students and produced award-winning one-act dramas. According to an actor in one of these companies, "the plays that were given closest attention were those that were immediately relevant...One of the prize-winning plays...dealt with apartheid in trains."[15]

Similar theatrical performances arose spontaneously in Soweto, the black suburb of Johannesburg, in the early 1960s. An account of some of these performances is worth quoting:

> Gibson Kente is one of the first people in Soweto who took to writing plays, and his first really popular play, *Sikalo*, took the townships by storm, since its theme was only too familiar to the inhabitants. Set in Soweto itself, the story is of a boy who grows up in the location, disregards his parents, becomes a thug, is arrested, and sentenced to be hanged. As usual, repentance comes too late. Kente has also written two other plays, *Lifa* and *Zwi*, which have not been nearly as popular as *Sikalo*.
>
> Another playwright who melodramatizes the life of the township is Samuel Mhangwana. His play, *The Unfaithful Woman*, received great acclaim and the theme, also township-based, is the infidelity of urban women. *Blame Yourself* is about a young man brought up in a deeply Christian atmosphere. But when he gets married, he leaves his uncle's house, falls prey to worldly snares, and consequently ruins his marriage. After much knocking about he returns to his wife, only to find that she has taken to illicit beer selling. In the end he takes his own life.
>
> Both Kente and Mhangwana make free use of township and gospel singing, which makes their plays very popular. The singing is usually accompanied by a lot of dancing, also peculiar to the townships. Because the themes grow out of the stuff of township life, the playwrights make free use of township jargon, and the jokes also have this flavour. At times they throw in some vernacular and Afrikaans slang, seemingly at random; that the audiences approve is shown by the frequency with which some expressions, or even lines, from the plays are freely quoted in the streets and on buses and trains. From what I have written it will be clear that the audiences are made up mainly of workers and the lower middle class, though I am far from suggesting that people with "higher" social pretensions shun these plays.[16]

Today such theatrical performances continue, some of them spiced with implicit political protest. The most popular plays deal with topical themes: color prejudice among blacks and coloureds, eviction of unmarried women and children from their township homes, the hazards and uncertainties of city life.[17] Wherever such entertainments go, they play to packed houses. In fact, theatre has become so popular in black South Africa that a specialized periodical called *S'ketsh': South Africa's Magazine for Popular Theatre and Entertainment* was started in 1972 to cater to the black play-going public.

Of course, censorship has already become an issue in township theatre. In 1975 Shafa'ath Ahmed Khan's play, "When You Mix Black with White," was banned by the government's new Publications Control Board because it dealt with a taboo topic – a love affair between a white woman and a black man.[18] Township playwrights also have to contend with the regulations laid down by local township censors who seem to be more preoccupied with getting rid of what is sexually explicit than what is politically suggestive. Several plays that have been passed by the Publications Control Board have been banned by the West Rand Bantu Administration Board because they violated certain of the following criteria:

there must be no nudity on stage
there must be no obscene language
plays must not criticize any officials
there must be no touching or exposing of private parts
love scenes must not be made to look realistic
there must be no bare breasts
skirts must be of decent length[19]

Black playwrights affected by this type of censorship have demanded to know why these same criteria have not been applied to plays written and staged by white playwrights in South Africa.

Recent events may have brought changes to the township stage. Considering all the riots and disruptions that have occurred in Soweto and other black communities in South Africa, one wonders what kind of plays are being performed there now. Have politics and sex been totally eliminated from these entertainments or has there been a resurgence of shocking realism? What kind of theatre emerges during a social revolution? Given the turbulence of the times, is popular drama in black South Africa likely to grow stronger or is it liable to suffer the same fate as popular fiction and popular poetry?

It is perhaps too early for a foreign observer to attempt to answer these questions, but the salient trends should define themselves in the coming years.[20] Whatever the outcome, it appears certain that some form of popular literary expression will continue to give voice to the dreams and nightmares of South African blacks. The last forty years have proved that a vital popular literature movement has the power and resilience to survive political oppression in a racist state.

NOTES

1. For a summary of early black literary activity in English, see Tim Couzens, "Black South African Literature in English, 1900-1950," in *Commonwealth Literature and the Modern World*, ed. Hena Maes-Jelinek (Brussels: Didier, 1975), pp. 89-96, and "The Continuity of Black Literature in South Africa before 1950," *English in Africa*, 1, 2 (1974), 11-23.

2. Two books have been written about this magazine by former editors: Anthony Sampson, *Drum* (London: Collins, 1956; Boston: Houghton Mifflin, 1957), and Tom Hopkinson, *In the Fiery Continent* (London: Gollancz, 1962).

3. For a fuller account of *Drum* fiction, see Ezekiel Mphahlele's remarks in Chapter 22 of his autobiography *Down Second Avenue* (reprint Garden City, N. Y.: Doubleday, 1971). Mphahlele worked as the literary editor of *Drum* from 1955 to 1957. For other accounts, see my "Post-War Literature in English by African Writers from South Africa: A Study of the Effects of Environment upon Literature," *Phylon*, 27 (1966), 50-62, and Don Dodson, "The Four Modes of *Drum*: Popular Fiction and Social Control in South Africa," *African Studies Review*, 17 (1974), 317-43.

4. This competition was started in 1952, *Drum*'s second year. By 1957 it was attracting more than 1600 entries. See *Drum* of May 1957 for an announcement concerning this popular annual competition.

5. Fred Hawkins, "Too Late to Love," *Drum*, October 1955, p. 49.

6. Tom Hopkinson, "Deaths and Entrances: The Emergence of African Writing," *The Twentieth Century*, 165 (1959), 333.

7. Duke Ngcobo, "Never Too Late for Love," *Drum*, September 1954, p. 41.

8. For a list of the stories published by black writers in *Drum, Our Africa, Zonk* and other South African publications, see my "A Preliminary Checklist of English Short Fiction by Non-Europeans in South Africa, 1940-1964," *African Studies Bulletin*, 12 (1969), 275-91.

9. Alfred Hutchinson, "Washerwoman Annie," *New Age*, 6 October 1955, p. 6.

10. T. H. Gwala, "The Knock," *New Age*, 22 January 1959, p. 4.

11. Anonymous serial stories such as "The Painted People," *Drum*, August-October 1964, and "The Spear vs. Dr. Satan," *Drum*, November 1964-January 1965, are typical of this period.

12. *Sounds of a Cowhide Drum* (Johannesburg: Renoster Books, 1971), p. 3.

13. Mongane Wally Serote, *Yakhal'inkomo: Poems* (Johannesburg: Renoster Books, 1972); James Matthews and Gladys Thomas, *Cry Rage!* (Johannesburg: Spro-cas Publications, 1972); Robert Royston, ed., *To Whom It May Concern: An Anthology of Black South African Poetry* (Johannesburg: Donker, 1973); James Matthews, ed., *Black Voices Shout!* (Athlone: BLAC Publishing House, 1974); Sydney Sipho Sepamla, *Hurry Up to It!* (Johannesburg: Donker, 1975); Mongane Wally Serote, *No Baby Must Weep* (Johannesburg: Donker, 1976).

14. *Black Voices Shout!*, p. 7.

15. Cosmo Pieterse, "Panel on South African Theater," *Issue*, 6, 1 (1976), 48.

16. Bernadette Mosala, "Theatre in Soweto," *Journal of Commonwealth Literature*, 8, 1 (1973), 64-65.

17. In addition to the articles in *S'ketsh'*, information on these plays can be found in 1975 issues of *Drum*. See, for instance, Joe Thloloe, "We're Out of Our Theatre Nappies," *Drum*, 8 March 1975, pp. 42-44, and Anon., "Mhangwana Tidies His *Unfaithful Woman*," *Drum*, 8 April 1975, pp. 60-61.

18. Anon., "When You Mix Black with White," *Drum*, 22 July 1975, pp. 38-39.

19. Anon., "Ban These Censors!" *Drum*, 22 July 1975, p. 19.

20.   One ominous sign is that the talented actors John Kani and Winston Ntshona were placed under house arrest some years ago and were forbidden to be seen in the company of more than five people, measures which momentarily curtailed their acting careers. See Caldwell Titcomb et al., "Silenced South Africans," *New York Review of Books*, 14 October 1976, p. 54.

Robin Hood Realism in South African Fiction

South African English fiction by Black and Coloured writers is infested with outlaw heroes. They come in all shapes and sizes – murderers, thieves, burglars, bank robbers, pickpockets, hoodlums, juvenile delinquents, gamblers, dope peddlers, bootleggers, shebeen queens, harlots, jail breakers, pass offenders, political agitators, revolutionaries – and most of them live extraordinarily violent lives in squalid urban slums, an environment that both makes and destroys them.

Several writers have tried to explain this preoccupation with outlaws, crime and violence. Ezekiel Mphahlele suggests that the non-white writer in South Africa is familiar with the world of the outlaw because he himself "lives inside violence, breathes it, feeds on it, whether it be vindictive or wanton. Robbery, murder, thuggery sum up his environment, where Negro fights against his own kind as well as against whites and even turns his violence upon himself."[1] Bloke Modisane sees the heroes of his own short stories as a projection of himself: "Like me, my characters were invested with a contempt for the law, their efforts were directed towards a flaunting of the law, my heroes were social maladjusts in a society where heroism is measured by acts of defiance against law and order."[2] Lewis Nkosi offers a psychological interpretation of the popularity of the outlaw, calling him a

> living symbol of that defiance against the social limits placed on the majority by a hateful regime which the middle class and ordinary workers would like to defy but have neither the courage, aptitude nor means with which to defy them. It is not by accident that in South Africa the Black middle class, including intellectuals and artists, accord the criminal who murders or robs white people the stature of a hero. In their most frustrated wishes he at once shows them the way and mocks their lack of dare. [3]

The fictional outlaw hero is thus a manifestation of racial discontent in South Africa, a sublimation of the urgent need of oppressed peoples to protest against things as they are.

Of course, not all fiction by South African non-whites is protest literature nor is all of it about outlaws. Even a good number of the outlaw stories are completely innocent of politics. For example, one occasionally finds humorous sketches of respectable pickpockets and gentlemanly crooks which are reminiscent of the underworld comedies of Damon Runyon.

Moreover, magazines such as *Drum* and *Zonk* which catered to an unsophisticated urban African audience made it their policy to publish the most sensational stories they could find, the gorier the better. So in the fifties and early sixties there was a lot of trashy pulp fiction churned out with a crime-does-not-pay theme which does not really deserve to be called protest literature.

Today it is virtually impossible to publish protest literature in South Africa because nearly all the liberal and radical publications which provided an outlet for it have been banned and other publications read and written by non-whites have been emasculated by stringent censorship provisions in the Publications and Entertainments Act of 1963. The most accomplished non-white writers have left the country and are now living and writing in exile. They continue to write protest literature but they must now address a foreign audience, for their works are invariably banned in South Africa.

Robin Hood Realism

The writers who have produced the most successful protest literature have employed a technique which can be called "Robin Hood realism." To explain what is meant by this term it will be necessary to review pertinent aspects of the Robin Hood legend. Robin Hood was an outlaw hero, a badman almost too good to be true. He did not hesitate to do a little evil (robbing the rich) in order to do a lot of good (giving to the poor). Because he was willing to break laws in order to relieve human suffering, he was a threat to the wealthy secular and religious Establishment and a champion to the down-trodden and oppressed peasantry. In modern parlance he was anti-bourgeois and pro-proletariat and he took the law into his own hands in order to effect a more equitable distribution of wealth. Today, he and his merry men would no doubt be regarded as a dangerous band of communist guerrillas.

But in his own time and place Robin Hood comes across as a very appealing figure, for it is quite clear that he is right and his world is wrong. No one could do so many good deeds and still be a villain. No one could be so brave, honest, noble, generous, courteous, kind and manly without being a hero. What's more, Robin Hood has a fine sense of humor and a boy scout's love of the outdoors. When he is not holding up noblemen and high churchmen, rescuing guiltless men from the gallows, or poaching the king's deer, he is relaxing in Sherwood Forest with his trusty followers, challenging them in archery contests and other sports. Robin Hood, in other words, is a clearly defined character in a clearly defined role.

Most important, Robin Hood does not attempt to explain or justify his role. We are never told why he decided to become an outlaw. There are no sermons preached about institutionalized injustice, social inequality, feudal oppression, economic exploitation, or ethnic discrimination. It is just assumed that he had good reason for choosing the career he did and that it was a wise choice. Since it is impossible to doubt his integrity, all blame must fall on his society. Robin Hood obviously lived in an immoral world, a world in which a good man, to remain good, had to become an outlaw. Presenting this paradox without fanfare, the Robin Hood legend is excellent protest literature.

The most effective protest literature by South African non-whites makes use of a similar strategy but a different technique. The hero is usually a good man who turns to crime in rebellion against an evil society. Or he might be an innocent, law-abiding individual who suffers hardships and indignities simply because he is a non-white in a white-dominated world. In either case, he is right and his world wrong. But unlike Robin Hood, he never triumphs in the end. However brave and good, he cannot beat the system or change the world. If he ventures to take the law into his hands, he is brutally crushed. He remains an underdog without a chance of coming out on top, a well-defined South African character in a well-defined South African role.

And he lives in an urban slum, not a sylvan glade. Immersed in a sea of filth, he seldom experiences beauty or tranquillity. His depressing environment is recorded in minute detail and without editorial comment. No shouts of protest are necessary, for the picture alone indicts the society which permits such inhumane conditions to exist. The protest is implicit rather than explicit.

This documentary manner of registering protest is also used effectively in descriptions of characters, actions, and events. The writer who fully exploits this technique to create a telling picture of the plight of the non-white underdog in South Africa and steadfastly resists the impulse to preach sermons and hand out propaganda will win rather than argue his readers over. As in the Robin Hood stories, all the right attitudes will be formed, all the right assumptions made. This is Robin Hood realism, the South African non-white writer's most potent form of protest.

Three South African Non-White Writers

Examples of effective and ineffective protest writing can be found in the works of three of South Africa's most prolific and accomplished non-white writers. In a rather melodramatic story in *Drum* about a political agitator in a Johannesburg slum Ezekiel Mphahlele has his hero say: "Put a man in a filthy place like this, you've condemned his soul to filth."[4] This is raw and blatant protest. The same idea is conveyed much more subtly and forcefully in another of Mphahlele's *Drum* stories, a humorous tale set in a similar slum community: "Nadia Street was reputed to be the quietest street in Newclare. Not that it is any different from other streets. It has its own dirty water, its own flies, its own horse manure; its own pot-bellied children with traces of urine down the legs."[5] Here the picture conveys the protest. No one has to stand up and shout the message to the reader. The details do all the work.

In Richard Rive's story "The Bench" an old Negro farmhand who has just heard a stirring anti-apartheid speech at a political rally decides he must assert his manhood by challenging one of his country's discriminatory laws. He sees a railway bench with "EUROPEANS ONLY" painted on it.

> For one moment it symbolized all the misery of the plural South Africa society. Here was his challenge to his rights as a man. Here it stood. A perfectly ordinary wooden bench, like hundreds of thousands of others in South Africa. His challenge. That bench now had concentrated in it all the evils of the system he could not understand. It was the obstacle between himself and humanity. If he sat on it he was a man. If he was afraid, he denied himself membership as a human in human society.[6]

Notice that Rive does not allow the bench or his hero's gesture to remain symbolic. Instead, he very carefully explains their significance so the reader will know exactly what to think and precisely how to feel. Rive tells so much and shows so little that his story becomes a lecture rather than a picture of South African society.

In a story entitled "The Return"[7] Rive adopts a different approach. A non-white stranger passing through a small South African village is refused drinking water by an Afrikaner housewife, is punched in the mouth by an aggressive white youth, and is forcibly ejected from a church for "whites only" during a sermon on "our duty to our neighbor." Not till the end of the story do we learn that the stranger is the returned Jesus. Rive does not vitiate the force of this trenchant ironic twist by smothering it in unnecessary explanations.

Like Mphahlele and Rive, Alex La Guma sometimes underscores his message with too heavy a hand. For example, in a story about a government pass office a white clerk is described as follows:

> A row of pens and pencils form a tiny fence across his breast, as if it had been erected there to keep out all feeling of friendliness, or even minute sparks of pity or compassion. He is unemotional, expressionless, a robot, part of the vast machinery created to enslave a people.[8]

La Guma also strains too hard to make his point in A Walk in the Night and And A Threefold Cord, his first two novels.[9]

But La Guma is South Africa's undisputed master of Robin Hood realism. Most of his heroes are men made criminals by their environment.

Underdogs, perpetual losers, victims of circumstance and unjust laws, they nevertheless possess a stubborn courage and a will to resist the forces that push them to the bottom. They are rebels with a social conscience.

La Guma's style is concrete, vivid, sometimes impressionistic, always documentary. Often his protest is conveyed entirely through verbal pictures. Here is a prison scene from his novel *The Stone Country*:

> The heat in the cell was solid. As Yusef the Turk would have said, you could reach out in front of your face, grab a handful of heat, fling it at the wall and it would stick. With over forty prisoners locked up in the middle of summer, the smell of sweat was heavy and cloying as the smell of death.[10]

This is the Coloured Section of the prison. In the White Section "the prisoners, most of them in shorts and bathing trunks, sunned themselves or chatted with the guards. There were very few of them, compared with the numbers in the other section."[11] The prison itself is described as

> a squat, wide girdle of brownstone and grey-painted mortar and concrete enclosing a straining body of brickwork and more stone.
> It had been built in the last century, during Victorian times, and over the years bits and pieces had been added to its interior, alterations made here and there, and because it could not expand outwards, it had closed in upon itself in a warren of cells, cages, corridors and styles.
> Outside, the facade had been brightened with lawns and flower-beds: the grim face of an executioner hidden behind a holiday mask. The brasswork on the castellated main door was polished to perfection, and the flagged pathway up to it, kept spotless, as if at any moment it would receive some dignitary or other. It waited like a diseased harlot, disguised in finery, to embrace an unsuspecting customer.[12]

Obviously the prison is a metaphor for South Africa. La Guma paints the picture and leaves the reader to draw the parallel.

In La Guma's fiction our sympathies are always with the underdog and the underdog is always non-white. However, not all non-whites are sympathetically portrayed. Those who take jobs as prison guards or policemen are considered sell-outs to the white world and those who rob and murder their own people are despised. La Guma does not stoop to tell the reader all this. He sets his characters in motion, stands back, and lets the reader judge for himself. La Guma's work is so skillfully done that the reader cannot fail to develop appropriate attitudes and make appropriate judgements.

La Guma's realism is quite a bit like the naturalism of American novelists such as Frank Norris, Theodore Dreiser and James Farrell. The hero is seen as an individual at the mercy of his environment and passions, a man who doesn't stand much of a chance unless he is well-adapted or willing to adapt to the particular set of circumstances in which he finds himself. However, La Guma differs from the American naturalists in his belief that man should struggle against his bonds, should seek to change his environment rather than adapt himself to it. He suggests that the South African underdog's only hope for a better future rests upon his willingness to continue his seemingly futile battle against the forces that hold him down. La Guma's outlaw heroes may never win but at least they never give up trying to win. They persist in the belief that man can change his universe and shape his future. Thus, deep in the heart of La Guma's realism runs a vein of pure romanticism.

NOTES

1. *The African Image* (London: Faber and Faber, 1962), p. 187.

2. *Blame Me on History* (New York: Dutton, 1963), p. 139.

3. "Alex La Guma: The Man and His Work," *South Africa: Information and Analysis*, 59 (January 1968), p. 3.

4. "Blind Alley," *Drum*, September 1963, p. 33.

5. "Down the Quiet Street," *Drum*, January 1956, p. 48.

6. *African Songs* (Berlin: Seven Seas, 1963), pp. 97-98.

7. *Ibid.*, pp. 103-15.

8. "The Machine," *Fighting Talk*, 12, 10 (October 1956), p. 8.

9. For discussion of these works, see my "Form and Technique in the Novels of Richard Rive and Alex La Guma," *Journal of the New African Literature and the Arts*, 2 (1966), pp. 10-15.

10. *The Stone Country* (Berlin: Seven Seas, 1967), p. 80.

11. *Ibid.*, p. 63.

12. *Ibid.*, p. 17.

Dennis Brutus's Mousey Tongue: People's Poetry in Exile

The "China Poems" of Dennis Brutus were inspired by his visit to mainland China late in the summer of 1973. During a six-week tour which took him to Peking, Hangchow, Shanghai and Canton, he decided to attempt to simulate in English the style of certain forms of Chinese poetic expression. He had composed short, simple lyrics previously, but never had he systematically reduced his verse to such spare, succinct utterances, never had he been so tight-fisted with words. In this parsimonious new idiom he sought to achieve an economy so extreme that the reader or hearer would have to supply most of the reverberations himself.

His model for this kind of verse was the poetry of Mao Tse-tung, which he had read in a new translation by Willis Barnstone and Ko Ching-Po shortly before going to China. Mao, he had learned, was "a major poet, an original master" in the classical tradition who did not place much value on his poetry, even though, like Brutus himself, he "had written poems obsessively, during years of wandering...writing all night, evening after evening, and then throwing away his 'scribbles'."[1] Captivated by the concentrated power of Mao's "scribbles," Brutus tried to discipline and refine his own lucid verse still further, paring it down to the barest essentials. In a note to his *China Poems* he explained, "Even before my trip I had begun to work towards more economical verse. My exposure to *haikus* and their tighter Chinese ancestors, the *chueh chu*, impelled me further.[2]

The Chinese verse form Brutus cites, the *chueh chu*, is described by Barnstone as:

> a four-line poem with five or seven characters in each line. It is the shortest poem in Chinese, and if the lines have only five characters each, the poem contains only twenty syllables. Like the Japanese *haiku*, it is the most compressed Chinese verse form, and from it came the *haiku*, which is three syllables shorter.[3]

Since Chinese characters are always monosyllabic and Chinese words are sometimes polysyllabic, "a four-character line might contain four, three, two words, or conceivably only one complete compound word."[4] In the rigorous *chueh chu*, as in all classical Chinese poetry, line length is determined by a fixed number of characters (i.e., syllables) per line, not a fixed number of words.

In experimenting with shorter and fewer lines in his own poetry, Brutus appears to have striven for a reduction in the total number of words per line and lines per poem without forcing the words and lines into a fixed metrical or syllabic pattern. He did not attempt to limit each line to a certain number of syllables but rather sought to achieve the more economical use of word, image and idea in tight, abbreviated lines. In other words, he was not seeking to render the *chueh chu* into English but only to emulate its verbal austerity. He has commented on the strategy behind such stringency:

> The trick is to say little (the nearer to nothing, the better) and to suggest much –
> as much as possible. The weight of meaning hovers around the words (which
> should be as flat as possible) or is brought by the reader/hearer. Non-emotive,
> near-neutral sounds should generate unlimited resonances in the mind; the
> delight is in the tight-rope balance between nothing and everything possible; be-
> tween saying very little and implying a great deal. Here are examples, from
> other sources, of this form.

> Goose-grey
> clouds
> lour

There is an enormous gap to be traversed in the mind between the softness (silliness is also suggested) of "goose-grey" and the thunderous menace of "lour" presaging a storm.

> Exile:
> schizophrenia
> suicide

Consider the terror of the journey to be made in the mind from exile to the declension of suicide.[5]

The two three-word poems cited here are not translations from ancient or modern Chinese verse but examples of the kind of extreme compression Brutus was hoping to achieve in English. Not even Mao himself (who apparently seldom used the *chueh chu* form)[6] had risked saying so little in his poems.

Brutus's *China Poems* are themselves not truly Chinese in structure or pattern. They are too free-moving, too irregular and sometimes too condensed or too expanded to be considered English equivalents of rigidly orthodox forms of classical Chinese verse. Brutus was evidently not interested in working within the strict formal constraints of the *chueh chu* or other oriental types of "regulated verse."[7] He sought merely to reduce his poems to flat, "non-emotive, near-neutral sounds" arranged as economically as possible on the page. Most of his "China Poems" are only three lines long, the exceptions being a few four- and seven-line lyrics. There are seldom more than four or five words to a line and sometimes only one or two. Moreover, the number of syllables per line is not fixed but varies considerably and appears to be governed by no immutable poetic laws. Rhyme and regular metre are consistently eschewed. In short, Brutus was writing truncated free verse, not English facsimiles of Chinese poetic forms.

This is not to say that his "China Poems" lack a Chinese orientation or flavor. Many of them contain references to specific places in China (e.g., the Long Wall, the People's Palace of Leisure, the new stadium in Shanghai) or to general features of the Chinese landscape (mountain ranges, earthworks, cornfields) which help to place the reader/hearer in the right geographical locale. Tributes to Chinese workers, to Mao and his first wife, and allusions to the "ruined palaces of Emperors" add appropriate political dimensions to lyrics in praise of Communist Chinese achievements. Such poems communicate exactly what Brutus hopes they would communicate: his "admiration for the Chinese people and their great leader, Mao Tse-tung."[8] They are Chinese in sympathy as well as subject matter.

Their brevity also gives them a deceptive oriental appearance, especially to the average Western reader whose acquaintance with oriental traditions of verse may be limited to English translations of Japanese *haiku*, short Chinese lyrics, and possibly the poems of Mao Tse-tung. Such readers may not be aware that Brutus's verse deviates radically from standard Chinese poetic forms. To the untrained eye, a paper tiger made with the wrong material might easily be mistaken for the real thing.

Of course, even counterfeit paper tigers may create genuine aesthetic excitement. Some of Brutus's "China Poems" are appealing not because they are successfully pseudo-Chinese, but because they can stand on their own as poetic utterances. Several, for instance, are deftly economical, achieving a terse eloquence which is pleasingly epigrammatic. Consider the following examples:

> It is to preserve
> beauty
> that we destroy.

> The Chinese carver
> building a new world:
> chips of ivory in his hair.

> At the Long Wall:
> a soldier
> holding a flower.

These poems operate on the principle of paradox, of unexpected and seemingly illogical leaps of thought or image which give the impression of being self-contradictory: we destroy in order to preserve; chips of an ancient art substance (ivory) play a part in building a new world; a soldier holds a flower. The tight-rope balance here appears to be between sense and nonsense, between premises at variance with conclusions. The initial images briefly build up expectations and the final image knocks them down. The imagination sets out on its journey and gets ambushed at the end. It is the ability of these poems to astonish and betray us that makes them successful.

There are also several vignettes among the Chinese poems which gain their strength from irony, the cousin of paradox.

> On the roofs
> of the ruined palaces of Emperors
> Imperial lions snarl
> at the empty air.

> The tree in the Emperor's Garden
> will not accept
> the discipline of marble.

It is easy to read political messages in these ironies, but different readers might be inclined to interpret them in different ways. For instance, the undisciplined tree in the Emperor's Garden could mean one thing to a Chinese Mainlander and something else to a Taiwanese. Explication of the image would depend entirely on one's point of view. Here is where extreme economy backfires on the economist. Or does it? Perhaps part of the strategy of generating "unlimited resonances in the mind" is to create ironies, ambiguities and contradictions which can never be completely resolved. A few well-chosen words could conceivably produce myriad tensions in the imagination. The poet would thus get maximum mental mileage with a minimum of gas. What he might lose in precision by such economy he would certainly regain in amplitude.

Not all of Brutus's "China Poems" achieve such heady inflation, however. Several fall so utterly flat that they cannot be resuscitated. A banal observation such as

> Peasants, workers
> they are the strength
> of the land.

never gets off the ground poetically, but is no worse than

> Miles of corn:
> it is simple:
> life is simple.

which is simply too simple for words. My favorite verbal void, however, is Brutus's toast at a sixty-course banquet in the Great Hall of the People, the Chinese Parliament. It consists of but six words, one of which is repeated three times:

> Good food
> good wine
> good friendship.

To which one is tempted to add, somewhat rudely, "but *not* good poetry." However, this isn't the only minipoem which is too prosaic to function as effective poetry.

> No task
> is impossible:
> Mao freed China.

reads more like a panegyrical platitude than a lyrical praise-poem. A longer effort such as:

> I have commuted between the world's capitals:
> travel is no longer an achievement;
> I must begin to do meaningful things.

lacks any kind of imaginative afflatus or poetic spirit. It merely sits on the page as a series of mundane ruminations. In such poems Brutus loses the lyrical momentum he has built up elsewhere in the collection by stringing together a series of resonant images.

In Chinese poetry, Barnstone tells us,

> It is an eye that sees an image, in present time...The eye sees with candor and reveals only what it sees. A simple yet complex lens. For in this poetry of observation are many depths of focus and a complexity of allusions. It is the reader who sees beyond the clear picture.[9]

In Brutus's flattest poems it is difficult for us to see beyond the clear picture. Indeed, at times it is difficult to see any picture at all because there are no concrete images on which we can fasten the energies of our imagination.

In Brutus's better poems this is not so. The opening sequence in "China Poems" offers the kind of "simple yet complex lens" with "many depths of focus" which allows us to see well beyond the images presented. The first poem in the sequence is an initial impression of China, a revealing snapshot taken on the road from Peking airport.

> Avenues of trees
> for miles:
> cicadas singing.

We experience this scene by seeing and hearing it. The trees appear to be geometrically arranged over immense distances; there is no anarchy of nature here. Man has conquered the environment, reorganized it agriculturally so it is more productive, and made efficient use of all available space. It is a well-cultivated landscape, man working in harmony with nature and rationally exploiting its resources. There is order and stability in such a world, the neat precision in the "avenues of trees for miles" suggesting that forces of disruption, inequity and imbalance have been subdued. Moreover, nature itself rejoices in the profound ecological change that has taken place; the cicadas sing because there is nothing for them to fear in this brave, new environment. They thrive and exult in their peaceful green universe. Thus, in addition to providing a graphic picture of a particular spot, the seven words of the poem imply that all's right in this Communist world. That may seem like quite a large message for a few words to carry but such is the power of the poem's suggestive imagery in the mind of at least one reader.

The next poem in the sequence has similar expansive power.

> Beyond the trees
> the limitless
> horizon.

This suggests not only an endless landscape, a vast and immeasurable panorama, but also an ever-receding horizon. One can see beyond the near and immediate to distant and future prospects. Everything is within the scope of one's ken. There are no obstacles or impediments to a vision which can embrace the entire world.

A political message is contained in this image, of course. Beyond this grove, beyond this well-ordered domain, beyond the People's Republic of China, lies the rest of the world, a horizon which offers unlimited opportunites for the extension of the Communist vision. The prospect is bright and hopeful because, from this vantage point, one can see no deterrents to the inevitable expansion of such an enlightened system. The future holds untold possibilities for spreading the Chinese outlook. Not even the sky is the limit!

The next poem reaffirms this notion by putting the subject in a new light:

> The sun is gone;
> only
> behind the near range.

In explaining this image to Ko Ching-Po, the translator of his poems, Brutus said:

> I am thinking of a mountain range – [the sun] is hidden but, in fact, one has no cause for despair because it is only because of the nearness of the mountain range [that is hidden]; In fact, the sun is still shining beyond that...I guess what is implicit there...is a sense of hope. One may be superficially and temporarily despondent but in fact one ought to be optimistic because the sun is shining. It's just that you can't see it for a while.[10]

In other words, though things may look dark and gloomy at times, one should take comfort in the knowledge that such moments are transitory. Sunshine, illumination, enlightenment continues somewhere in the world and will return soon. Despite the near range of mountains which obscures the realities of one's true situation from time to time, the horizon is still limitless, the vistas still clear and conquerable, the Communist vision of a better world still possible. Indeed, the sun is already shining elsewhere to the west. Any temporary setback should therefore be viewed in its proper perspective. A brief eclipse of the sun does not mean the world is coming to an end. The sun may have set momentarily, but the sun also rises.

There is, of course, a South African dimension to this sequence of poems, as there tends to be in most of Brutus's poetry. Mainland China has undergone its revolution; South Africa has not yet done so. In talking about limitless horizons and transitory setbacks, Brutus is suggesting that the revolutionary struggle that was won in China can also be won elsewhere. If there are moments of despair or doubt, one should remember that the dawn is soon coming, that the cicadas will someday be singing in other radically transformed gardens of the world.

There may be additional ways to interpret these poems that would amplify their range of semantic significance still further. Other readers will doubtless find other meanings embedded in the same lines. "The trick," as Brutus puts it, "is to say little...and to suggest much – as much as possible." In this opening sequence of poems the trick works splendidly.

But it does not always work – at least not for every reader. Certain of Brutus's China poems, even though filled with graphic images, do not stimulate the imagination adequately. Here is one describing "A People's Commune":

> Earthworks covered with moss,
> an empty goldfish bowl,
> a piglet, a melon.

This sequence of four images may have been intended to stir up a vision of rustic innocence but the images are too disparate, too unconnected, to form a coherent picture. The poem becomes a meaningless inventory of phenomena with no clear message to communicate. It could as easily be construed as a criticism of communal inactivity (mossy earthworks, empty goldfish bowl, a piglet the only sign of animate life in an otherwise stagnant and sterile environment) as a commendation of peasant simplicity.

Brutus actually hoped the poem would convey a very favorable image of a typical Chinese commune. He told his translator he had deliberately chosen to make the poem very simple because

> It's really trying to talk about the calm, the placidness, the contentment and joy that you can find in the commune. Everything is tranquil and there's no conflict or tension, and I'm trying to communicate this feeling with just observing what is there...One may have something for recreation like a goldfish bowl but if you no longer had the goldfish in the bowl, it wouldn't matter. You don't have a thirst for display or for possession.[11]

This romantic view of a utopian communal existence is not successfully evoked by the images Brutus selects. The poem says far less than the poet wants it to say.

All of Brutus's China poems are experiments in economical communication. Sometimes they succeed, sometimes they fail, but even the most dismal failures are interesting as attempts to make a few neutral words yield a great deal of meaning. Any poet who tries to achieve such resonant compression runs the risk of squeezing all vitality out of his verse and being left with only a handful of dry banalities. It is to Brutus's credit that he occasionally succeeds in making an exceedingly short string of words sing. His China Poems may not be his best verse but they are far from his worst, and they reveal that he is still actively seeking new ways to express his lyrical impulse.

NOTES

1. Willis Barnstone and Ko Ching-Po, eds. and trs. *The Poems of Mao Tse-tung.* (Toronto, New York, London: Bantam Books, 1972), pp. 21-22.

2. Dennis Brutus, *China Poems* (Austin: African and Afro-American Studies and Research Center, 1975), p. 35. All poems quoted are from this edition.

3. Barnstone, p. 159.

4. *Ibid.*, p. 157. For a more technical discussion of the *chueh chu*, see Harold Shadick and Ch'iao Chien, *A First Course in Literary Chinese*, Vol. III (Ithaca and London: Cornell University Press, 1968), pp. 571-72; and Burton Watson, *Chinese Lyricism* (New York and London: Columbia University Press, 1971), pp. 111-12, 145-47.

5. Brutus, p. 35.

6. Not one of the poems included in Barnstone's collection appears to assume this form.

7. For a brief discussion of the main types, see Barnstone, pp. 157-59.

8. Brutus, p. 5.

9. Barnstone, p. 3.

10. Tape recording of a telephone conversation between Dennis Brutus and Ko Ching-Po, January 30, 1975.

11. *Ibid.*

Seeing the Races Through Zulu Spectacles

In two of the most popular films of 1977, "Star Wars" and "Close Encounters of the Third Kind," the audience is taken on a journey of the imagination and introduced to some of the inhabitants of outer space. These beings, who strike us as weird because they do not conform to the familiar behavioral patterns of earthly Homo sapiens, are also quite fearsome because they have managed to harness powerful forces of nature over which human beings in the last quarter of the twentieth century exercise no control. They are both unpredictable and technologically advanced – a dangerous combination as far as the ordinary viewer is concerned. One feels threatened by the superior intelligence and questionable morality of such creatures for one cannot anticipate what they are likely to do with their formidable powers.

In "Star Wars" we also see some lower forms of life – huge, lumbering reptilian monsters; diminutive sand people; a hairy, ape-like wookie; anatomically variegated saloon bums; and robots of every conceivable design – but they seem less intimidating because they can be easily outwitted or else destroyed by remarkable new weaponry. Like the Indians in most westerns, like the bizarre animals, insects or half-human brutes in many horror tales, the lower-class cosmic fauna in science fiction ultimately end up at the mercy of "civilized" man. They may offer us a few thrills by threatening to get out of hand from time to time, but their primary function in our imaginative life seems to be to validate our conception of ourselves as superior beings capable of keeping elemental forces under our control. We appear to have a very compelling need to believe that we are better and stronger creatures than others.

Five centuries before the first Sputnik launched our exploration of the closest layers of outer space, opening those realms to attempts at confirmation of our imaginative projections, western man developed the technology necessary to make long voyages at sea, thereby facilitating the exploration of a world of nearer space. Suddenly, with the first circumnavigations of the globe, different peoples were put in touch with one another on a scale never previously possible. These initial contacts stimulated a great deal of curiosity about the variety of the human species, and ships often brought live specimens from remote ports to prove the truth of travelers' tales. The most cosmopolitan centers in Europe, particularly London and Paris, became depots for these exotic goods which usually were displayed to the public for a small fee. But this great side-show of humanity did not dispel the myopic ethnocentrism of the viewers, even after several centuries of face-to-face exposure to other ways of being. Rather, it tended to have the opposite effect. A Londoner or Parisian, seeing a Bushman, Cherokee, Eskimo or Australian Aborigine for the first time, might have been struck by the novelty of his appearance but would not have been tempted to consider him an equal in intelligence or sophistication. Indeed, such a sight probably would have made him grateful that he had been born a European amply blessed with all the benefits of living in a "higher" civilization. Cultural superiority was assumed to be in no need of proof. The "savage," noble or ignoble, was evidence enough that Western man had climbed a long way up the ladder of human evolution.

In this essay I intend to examine several close encounters of this absurd kind, the first of which occurred when a performing troupe of thirteen Zulus were brought to London in 1853 by A. T. Caldecott, a prosperous merchant from Pietermaritzburg. Caldecott, an 1820 settler in South Africa, had long desired "that the English public should be gratified with a sight of the interesting savages, by whom he was surrounded in the fertile and flourishing colony of Natal,"[1] and had gone to considerable trouble and expense to convey this group of them to England by steamer in order to display them in an impressively mounted exhibition at a Hyde Park Corner theatre. If his motives were as much monetary as educational, it can be said that he succeeded on all fronts, for the Zulus turned out to be a smash hit and later went on to tour France, Germany and possibly some of the English provinces.

Of course, there was good reason to suppose that the English public would be curious about the Zulus. Tales of this "warlike" people and their "bloodthirsty" leaders Shaka and Dingaan had been filtering back to the British Isles for more than thirty years, and in the decade that followed England's annexation of a part of Zululand as the Colony of Natal in 1843, thousands of British settlers had emigrated there. Kith and kin back home no doubt wanted to see natives from this troubled corner of the empire for themselves.

But even without their reputation for bloodcurdling ferocity, the Zulus would have been an interesting novelty in Victorian England. Blacks had been seen in London for centuries and were becoming quite numerous in the city by the middle of the nineteenth century, but most of them were ex-slaves from North America or the West Indies – blacks, in other words, who had become Westernized to some extent. True Africans and other so-called "primitive peoples" were still a relatively rare sight in most European capitals and were exhibited as biological sports, analogous to unique tropical specimens in a botanical garden or metropolitan zoo. The science of ethnology was just getting established in Britain in the 1840s, and learned professors as well as uneducated laymen would flock to these exhibitions to study the latest arrivals from exotic lands overseas. A great sensation had been made earlier in the century by a bottom-heavy young lady from South Africa, popularly known as the "Hottentot Venus," who had been displayed throughout Europe confined in a cage and paraded on a chain.[2] During the months the Zulus were on stage in London, there were competing shows of such peoples as the "Earthmen" (supposedly "pigmies from Southern Africa" who lived in holes in the ground)[3] and the "Aztec Lilliputians" (later exposed as hoaxes, being nothing more than profoundly retarded and deformed children put on display by mercenary hucksters).[4] Yet each of these unusual groups – Earthmen, Aztec Lilliputians, and Zulus – was honored by being summoned to give a command performance at Buckingham Palace for Queen Victoria and her children. They were anthropological curiosities sought out by Crown and commoner alike.

What helped to make the Zulu exhibition more popular than the others was its theatrical dimension; the Zulus offered an extremely dramatic performance, not a static sideshow. Caldecott's troupe acted out incidents said to be typical of Zulu life and did so with great energy. To explain some of the scenes, Caldecott's son served as interpreter and master of ceremonies, lecturing briefly on Zulu customs and traditions before they were enacted on the stage.[5]

The earliest review of the "Caffres at Hyde-Park-Corner" (as they came to be known), appeared in the *Times* two days after their maiden performance. It is worth quoting in full because it is typical of the response of British theatre critics to this novel entertainment:

> Although there have been several attempts to render Caffre life familiar to the English public through the medium of exhibitions, nothing in this way had been done so completely or on so large a scale as the new exhibition opened Monday evening in the rooms formerly occupied by the Chinese Museum. Eleven Zulu men, with a woman and a child, are assembled into a company, and instead of performing one or two commonplace feats, they may be said to go through the whole drama of Caffre life, while a series of scenes, painted by Mr. Charles Marshall, gives an air of reality to the living pictures. Now the Caffres are at their meal, feeding themselves with enormous spoons, and expressing their satisfaction by a wild chant, under the inspiration of which they bump themselves along without rising in a sort of circular dance. Now the witchfinder commences his operations to discover the culprit whose magic has brought sickness into the tribe, and becomes perfectly rabid through the effect of his own incantations. Now there is a wedding ceremony, now a hunt, now a military expedition, all with characteristic dances; and the whole ends with a general conflict between

rival tribes. The songs and dances are, as may be expected, monotonous in the extreme, and without the bill it would be difficult to distinguish the expression of love from the gesture of martial defiance. Nevertheless, as a picture of manners, nothing can be more complete; and not the least remarkable part of the exhibition is the perfect training of the wild artists. They seem utterly to lose all sense of their present position, and, inspired by the situations in which they are placed, appear to take Mr. Marshall's scenes for their actual abode in the vicinity of Port Natal. If 11 English actors could be found so completely to lose themselves in the characters they assumed, histrionic art would be in a state truly magnificent. [6]

Other reviewers singled out many of the same features for comment – the excellent scenery, the impressive physical appearance of the Zulus, the spirited and uninhibited acting. A columnist for *The Athenaeum* spoke of the "almost perfect dramatic effect with which these wild men play their parts,"[7] and a reviewer for *The Spectator*, equally impressed with the "considerable dramatic propriety" of the performances, praised the vigor of the acting:

The charm-song and the proceedings of the witchfinder or "smeller out" were especially expressive and forcible in their pantomine. As for the noises – the howls, yells, hoots, and whoops, the snuffling, wheezing, bubbling, grovelling, and stamping – they form a concert to whose savagery we cannot attempt to do justice. [8]

The Illustrated London News initially described the exhibition simply as a "picturesque drama [consisting of] a series of scenes which charm by their spirit and *vraisemblance*" and often excite laughter by depicting incidents "more amusing than anything in a farce,"[9] but in its next issue it printed a sketch of one of the scenes in the show, gave brief biographical details on several of the performers, and elaborated on what it had found particularly entertaining:

After a supper of meal, of which the Kaffirs partake with their large wooden spoons, an extraordinary song and dance are performed, in which each performer moves about on his haunches, grunting and snorting the while like a pair of asthmatic bellows...but no description can give an idea of the cries and shouts – now comic, now terrible – by which the Kaffirs express their emotions. The scene illustrative of the preliminaries of marriage and the bridal festivities might leave one in doubt which was the bridegroom, did not that interesting savage announce his enviable situation by screams of ecstasy which convulse the audience. The Zulus must be naturally good actors; for a performance more natural and less like acting is seldom if ever seen upon any stage.[10]

The "Zulu Kaffir Exhibition" was obviously good theatre and deserved to become a huge box-office success.

On May 26th, after the show had been on for a week and a half and the first rave reviews had appeared, Charles Dickens went to see it, inviting his friend John Leech to accompany him.[11] Dickens may have been in need of relaxation for he was terribly overworked at the time. Not only was he writing the final chapters of *Bleak House* in monthly installments as well as the middle chapters of *A Child's History of England* but in addition he was busy editing *Household Words*, a popular weekly journal he had launched in 1850. As might be expected in such circumstances, the Zulus turned out to be more than mere transitory entertainment for him; they became grist for his prolific mill. Shortly after witnessing their performance, he wrote a humorous essay entitled "The Noble Savage" which appeared in the June 11th issue of *Household Words*. Though he made reference to such people as the "Ojibbeway" Indians and the Bushmen who had been on display in London earlier, he focussed his attention principally on Caldecott's Zulus, using them as hilarious examples of the ignobility of uncivilized man. The essay has been called "one of the most effective philippics of our language,"[12] and there can be no doubt that Dickens, with his incomparable flair for comic exaggeration, achieved his aim of debunking the Romantic myth of the "noble savage." Here are a few samples:

> Though extremely ugly, [the Zulus] are much better shaped than such of their predecessors as I have referred to; and they are rather picturesque to the eye, though far from odoriferous to the nose. What a visitor left to his own interpretings and imaginings might suppose these noblemen to be about, when they give vent to that pantomic expression which is quite settled to be the natural gift of the noble savage, I cannot possibly conceive; for it is so much too luminous for my personal civilisation that it conveys no idea to my mind beyond a general stamping, ramping, and raving, remarkable (as everything in savage life is) for its dire uniformity...

> If [a Zulu] wants a wife he appears before the kennel of the gentlemen whom he has selected for his father-in-law, attended by a party of male friends of a very strong flavor, who screech and whistle and stamp an offer of so many cows for the young lady's hand. The chosen father-in-law – also supported by a high-flavored party of male friends – screeches, whistles, and yells (being seated on the ground, he can't stamp) that there never was such a daughter in the market as his daughter, and that he must have six more cows. The son-in-law and his select circle of backers, screech, whistle, stamp, and yell in reply, that they will give three more cows. The father-in-law (an old deluder, overpaid at the beginning) accepts four, and rises to bind the bargain. The whole party, the yound lady included, then falling into epileptic convulsions, and screeching, whistling,

stamping, and yelling together – and nobody taking any notice of the young lady (whose charms are not to be thought of without a shudder) – the noble savage is considered married, and his friends make demoniacal leaps at him by way of congratulation...

The noble savage sets a king to reign over him, to whom he submits his life and limbs without a murmur or question, and whose whole life is passed chin deep in a lake of blood; but who, after killing incessantly, is in turn killed by his relations and friends, the moment a gray hair appears on his head. All the noble savage's wars with his fellow-savages (and he takes no pleasure in anything else) are wars of extermination – which is the best thing I know of him, and the most comfortable to my mind when I look at him. He has no moral feelings of any kind, sort, or description; and his "mission" may be summed up as simply diabolical...

After more examples of this sort, Dickens concludes his argument by stating:

My position is, that if we have anything to learn from the Noble Savage, it is what to avoid. His virtues are a fable; his happiness is a delusion; his nobility, nonsense...and the world will be all the better when his place knows him no more. [13]

Although it sometimes appears so in this essay, Dickens was not really recommending genocide. He was very much the Victorian pragmatist striving to puncture an inflated Romantic conception of the dignity of primitive peoples. The Zulus were simply a convenient case in point, a group so far removed from Europe in custom and culture that they could easily be held up as examples of a benighted race desperately in need of enlightenment. Dickens was not serious when he suggested that such peoples be exterminated; rather, he wanted them "civilised off the face of the earth."[14] He believed in cultural, not literal, genocide.

Yet it is interesting to note with what contempt Zulu customs, traditions and institutions were viewed by the London audiences who saw Caldecott's troupe perform. The performers obviously overstepped the boundaries of Victorian decorum when they sang and danced, but their antics presumably would not have provoked so much hilarity among spectators with cultural traditions more closely akin to those of the performers themselves. Underlying the reaction of Dickens and other English viewers was a broad streak of undisguised racism, a belief that the Zulus were morally and mentally inferior to Europeans. The numerous comments on their smell, their bizarre modes of dress (and undress), their noises, their monotonous songs, rabid incantations, and wild, demoniacal dances, betray an arrogant assumption that the Zulus were overgrown children of nature who had not yet developed the inhibitions, self-discipline and manners that distinguish more civilized folk. They were savages pure and simple, primitives in the raw.

Of course, one cannot really blame the Victorians for being so ethnocentric. Nineteenth century Europe, with its numerous civil and international wars, was not exactly a showcase of ethnic tolerance, and inadequate opportunities for face-to-face cultural contact with the non-Western world hindered Europeans from learning much about the human beings who inhabited the rest of the globe. There were no documentary films or television specials then to bring more accurate images of foreign peoples to the drawing rooms of London. The Zulus were therefore merely a spectacle, a carnival act consciously designed to play up their abnormalities – i.e., their radical deviance from European norms of dress and behavior. It would be ethnocentric of us to expect audiences who saw them 125 years ago to react with a more modern sensibility and to come away from such a performance with a richer understanding and appreciation of Zulu culture.

Indeed, one wonders if this would be possible in Europe or America even today. There is strong evidence to suggest that it would not. If we examine the reviews of more recent black South African performances in London and New York, we find remarkable echoes of those antiquated Victorian attitudes. Dickens is obviously not dead yet.

More than a century elapsed before a second black South African musical managed to reach the London stage. This was *King Kong*, a jazz opera set in Johannesburg shantytowns, which ran for more than eight months at Princess Theatre in 1961. Though the script was written and produced by white South Africans, though the setting was urban rather than rural, though the hero was an Othello-like boxer who strangled the woman he loved and then committed suicide, drama critics yielded to the temptation to fasten on what seemed to be the crudest aspects of an animated performance. The London *Times* called it a "piece of naive but vital indigenous art" and went on to say:

> The naivety, the rhythm and the vitality have a characteristic colour and manner of their own. They seem to be conditioned by the particular locality to which the characters belong; and it is perfectly easy to take what appears to us as stage clumsiness in our stride and to yield ourselves up to the rhythm and the vitality.
>
> Mostly the dances are frankly erotic, with the dancers using their hips and legs, or they are war dances with the gangsters seeking to strike terror with their foot movements. The songs are always strongly, if seldom melodiously, sung …There is also a wildly uninhibited gangster dance culminating in a murder and an enchanting wedding hymn warmly lit and beautifully dressed which also culminates in a murder.[15]

Except for the gangsters, this almost sounds like a revival of the "Caffres at Hyde-Park-Corner."

King Kong was a harbinger of things to come. In recent years no fewer than four Zulu musicals have been brought to London, and all have received similar reviews. In 1972 *Umabatha*, an attempt to tell the story of Chaka as a super-sanguinary Macbeth, met with this startled response:

> Before the murder, Mbatha (Macbeth) takes snuff and sneezes; an approved method of achieving second sight, which brings him the vision of an assegai. His letter to his wife is communicated as a drum message. And the three witches are transformed into *sangomas* (witchdoctors) who upset all Western notions of the sinister by conducting jolly dances round the cauldron shaking with seemingly innocent laughter. The most surprising thing about the whole show is its apparent good humour...
>
> The dances are built on a uniform beat to a short melodic fragment, and when one of these ostinatos starts building up the stage really catches fire. The shields go down to the ground while a leader whirls demonically in the foreground, executing high-kicks up to his chin, and bringing in the group with a pounding one-footed beat.
>
> The effect is as stunning visually as it is to listen to: a mass of moving skins and weapons transforming separate members into a single indomitable animal, bent on celebration, joy, or killing, but unstoppable no matter what its objective.[16]

Singing, dancing, and drumming were also singled out as the most impressive features of *Kwa Zulu*, a musical that opened in London in July, 1975.[17] But an even more enthusiastic response greeted the musical gyrations in *Ipi-Tombi*, which premiered a few months later. The *Times* called it "all ululating leaps, steatopygous flourishes, and tableaux of warriors framed in russet skybroth silhouette" which added up to "an evening of exotic escape."[18] The *Sunday Times* went further, hailing it as a

> thrilling production, presented with a verve, an *éclat*, a technical brilliance, a richness of voice in the singing, an excitement and a precision in the dancing which I do not believe that even the best American musical could rival. It is a riot of colour and movement, yet it is as controlled as the changing of the Guard. Every member of the huge cast is superb.[19]

Ipi-Tombi did not win such unrestrained applause when it travelled to New York in January, 1977. The fact that the show was picketed by anti-apartheid groups may have made some critics think twice about the political significance of the atmosphere of joy, happiness, and innocence being conveyed by the black performers, but it did not stop a few reviewers from indulging in the usual cliches about African atavism. The dances, *Time* magazine exclaimed, illustrate how close to nature some Africans apparently still are. The gestures, the rhythms, and the sounds indicate an unbroken totemic relationship with animals. The members of the troupe slither like snakes, stalk like the great cat family of the jungle, stamp and trumpet like elephants. This is all done with an agility, grace and energy that is breathtaking. The lead drummer (Junior Tshabalala) plays with galvanic fervor and propels the best number in the show, a warrior dance, into a Dionysian frenzy.[20]

Dickens would have loved it. Such a performance would have proved to him that savages are no nobler now that they were 125 years ago, thereby reinforcing his belief that "between the civilized European and the barbarous African there is a great gulf set."[21]

Perhaps it is stretching a point to compare Zulu performers in London and New York to the lower order of creatures who "people" science fiction films, but it must be admitted that they have a lot in common. Both are spectacularly odd and fearsome, but we do not fear them. Both can be cute and even lovable on occasion, but we do not really love them. Both are wild and powerful, but we control them, if only in our fantasies. Their unorthodox behavior underscores their difference from us, thereby validating our own way of being as normal and sensible. We need them in order to purchase a better opinion of ourselves. If Zulus were more recognizably human on stage, we might be challenged to accept them, at least in imagination, as our brothers and sisters. But when they sing, dance and drum as demonically as they do, then obviously they come from a different world and must be kept in their proper place, always a good distance from us. Such performers, no matter how entertaining – indeed, no matter how necessary and potentially beneficial to our mental health – serve to increase the great gulf of misunderstanding between Europeans and Africans and thus perpetuate the pathology of racism.

NOTES

1.   C. H. Caldecott, *Descriptive History of the Zulu Kafirs, Their Customs and Their Country, with Illustrations* (London: John Mitchell, 1853), p.4.

2.   Percival R. Kirby, "The Hottentot Venus," *Africana Notes and News*, 6, 3 (1949), 55-62, and "More about the Hottentot Venus," *Africana Notes and News*, 10, 4 (1953), 124-34.

3.   "Earthmen from Port Natal," *Illustrated London News*, 6 November 1852, pp. 371-72.

4.   *The Examiner*, 9 July 1853, p. 439; *Journal of Ethnological Science*, 4 (1856), 120-37, 297.

5.   This lecture was made available in published form under the title given in footnote 1, above.

6.   London *Times*, 18 May 1953, p. 8.

7.   *The Athenaeum*, 28 May 1853, p. 650.

8.   *The Spectator*, 21 May 1853, p. 485.

9. *The Illustrated London News*, 21 May 1853, p. 399.
10. *The Illustrated London News*, 28 May 1853, p. 409.
11. See letter of 23 May 1853 in the *Nonesuch Dickens*, Vol. 2 (London: Nonesuch Press, 1937), pp. 462-63.
12. W. Walter Crotch, *The Touchstone of Dickens* (London: Chapman and Hall, 1920), p. 85.
13. "The Noble Savage," *Household Words*, 11 June 1853, pp. 337-39.
14. *Ibid.*, p. 337.
15. London *Times*, 24 February 1961, p. 17.
16. London *Times*, 4 April 1972, p. 6.
17. See the reviews in the London *Times*, 25 August 1975, p. 7, and the *Sunday Times*, 3 August 1975, p. 24.
18. London *Times*, 20 November 1975, p. 10.
19. *Sunday Times*, 23 November 1975, p. 35.
20. *Time*, 24 January 1977, p. 56. The fourth Zulu musical of the 1970's *Uhlanga*, was panned by the press; see, e.g., London *Times*, 6 January 1977, p. 11, and *Sunday Times*, 9 January 1977, p. 37.
21. Charles Dickens, "The Niger Expedition," *Miscellaneous Papers*, Vol. I (New York: Charles Scribner & Sons, 1908), p. 133.